# Becoming Free Indeed

# Becoming Free Indeed

## MY STORY OF DISENTANGLING
## FAITH FROM FEAR

## JINGER DUGGAR VUOLO

### WITH COREY WILLIAMS

W PUBLISHING GROUP

AN IMPRINT OF THOMAS NELSON

Published in Nashville, Tennessee, by W Publishing, an imprint of Thomas Nelson.

The author is represented by Alive Literary Agency.

Thomas Nelson titles may be purchased in bulk for educational, business, fundraising, or sales promotional use. For information, please email SpecialMarkets@ThomasNelson.com.

Unless otherwise noted, Scripture quotations are taken from the ESV® Bible (The Holy Bible, English Standard Version®). Copyright © 2001 by Crossway, a publishing ministry of Good News Publishers. Used by permission. All rights reserved.

Scripture quotations marked DRA are taken from the Douay-Rheims 1899 American Edition. Public domain.

Scripture quotations marked KJ21 are taken from the 21st Century King James Version. Copyright © 1994 by Deuel Enterprises, Inc. Used by permission.

Scripture quotations marked KJV are taken from the King James Version. Public domain.

Scripture quotations marked NASB are taken from the New American Standard Bible® (NASB). Copyright © 1960, 1962, 1963, 1968, 1971, 1972, 1973, 1975, 1977, 1995, 2020 by The Lockman Foundation. Used by permission. www.lockman.org

Scripture quotations marked NASB1995 are taken from the New American Standard Bible® (NASB). © 1960, 1971, 1977, 1995 by The Lockman Foundation. Used by permission. www.Lockman.org. All rights reserved. Some personal names and identifying details have been changed to protect the privacy of the individuals involved.

Any internet addresses, phone numbers, or company or product information printed in this book are offered as a resource and are not intended in any way to be or to imply an endorsement by Thomas Nelson, nor does Thomas Nelson vouch for the existence, content, or services of these sites, phone numbers, companies, or products beyond the life of this book.

ISBN 978-1-4003-3584-8 (audiobook)
ISBN 978-1-4003-3583-1 (eBook)
ISBN 978-1-4003-3581-7 (HC)

Library of Congress Control Number: 2022944352

*Printed in the United States of America*

23 24 25 26 27  LBC  8 7 6 5 4

*To those who have been hurt by the teachings
of Bill Gothard or any religious leader who
claimed to speak for God but didn't*

. . . a bruised reed he will not break,
and a faintly burning wick he will not quench;
he will faithfully bring forth justice.

ISAIAH 42:3

# Contents

# Introduction

*I first had* the idea to write this book in the summer of 2017. My husband, Jeremy, and I had just attended an Advanced Training Institute conference in Big Sandy, Texas (later in the book, I'll talk more about what the conference is and why we went). While there, I saw dozens of people I'd grown up with—friends who, like me, had come to Big Sandy every year. But for every old friend I saw that week, there was one or two I expected to see who didn't show up. In the coming months and years, I'd start to hear stories of those friends. I'd find out that some of them no longer loved Jesus and wanted nothing to do with Christianity. As they reached young adulthood, they had rejected everything they'd been taught about God, the Bible, and the Christian faith.

While that is not my story—I am a Christian who loves Jesus and wants to follow Him—I have, like those friends, rejected much of the teaching I heard each year at the conference in Big Sandy. My faith is still intact, but it has changed. Instead of leaving the faith entirely, I have unthreaded, or disentangled, the truth of Christianity from the unhealthy version I heard growing up. My hope is that this book will be a help to my friends who are struggling to see who Jesus truly is. They were taught harmful and destructive teachings that have nothing to do with the grace of Jesus. They thought that was what Christianity was all about. But it isn't.

I also hope this book can be helpful for those who are still following those teachings. When you grow up in a tight-knit community where everyone believes the same things about everything—not just who God is but also how men and women are supposed to dress and speak—it's hard to even consider the possibility that what you were taught was wrong. My prayer is that this book will help you—no matter what community you grew up in or what you were taught—learn how to honestly examine your beliefs and know whether they are the same as what God says. I hope that the teachers you leaned on when you were younger pointed you to Jesus. But I know that's not always the case. Thankfully, many people pointed me to Christ, but I leaned heavily on one teacher who rarely did. And so, I'm hopeful my story can be helpful if you realize someone you've been looking to for wisdom is lacking the wisdom you need most.

Finally, I want this book to bring many of you into my life beyond the television show. I'm thankful for the millions of people who have watched my family over the years—who saw me grow up. I know that many of you do not believe the same things I do about God and the Bible. I invite you into my life so you can see that through the highs and lows, the trials my family has endured, and the changes in what I believe and how I live, that Jesus is my strength. He is worthy. I pray this book will help you see why I follow Him.

As I began to write this book, I realized that I needed help. I am not a professional writer. I'm not an expert on the Bible. I know what I believe and what I want to say, but I'm not always the best at expressing it. So I asked a friend of mine, Corey Williams, to help. He's a gifted writer and a student of the Bible who has helped me articulate what I believe in a way that I hope is helpful for you.

While this is not the first book I've written, it is the most challenging. The process has been far more emotionally exhausting than I thought it would be. It's been tough because it's so personal. At times, I've wondered if I should even write it. But I know it's necessary. I am thankful God has given me the strength to finish it. I want you to know at the start that this book is not a tell-all. It is not a critique of my childhood. I had a wonderful childhood. My parents loved me and sacrificed so much for me. For all of us. They invested their time and energy and souls into raising me and my brothers and sisters. Their patience, kindness, and love are things I want to imitate in raising my girls. They pointed me to Jesus. So this is not a book about them. I love my mom, dad, and entire family. This is a book about me and my spiritual journey. It is the story of my faith and how I've had to figure out what I believe and why I believe it. This is my personal theological memoir. Thanks for coming along for the journey.

# CHAPTER 1

# Growing Up in a Fishbowl

*Here's one of* the many quirky facts about being a Duggar: my husband, Jeremy, and I didn't watch our first movie together until we were husband and wife. On our honeymoon in 2016, we watched *The Truman Show*. I had never seen it before. (That's something I can say about *a lot* of movies!)

You probably already know that *The Truman Show* is about the ultimate fishbowl. The main character, Truman Burbank, is the star of a reality TV show, but he doesn't know it. Every moment of his life is captured for television. He lives inside a dome in Burbank, California, but he thinks he lives in a place called Seahaven Island. Many people from the outside world have opinions and expectations about who Truman should be and how he should live. Truman marries a woman the producers pick for him—not the woman he loves. The producers also pick his job and decide where he will live and who his best friend will be. When Truman begins to question his reality and tries to get out of Seahaven, his escape is blocked at every turn.

After we finished the movie, I turned to Jeremy and said, "That movie is my life." Well, except for the spouse-picking part.

I've been on television since I was ten years old. In 2004, Discovery Health Channel aired a documentary about my family called *14 Children and Pregnant Again*, which was followed by three more documentaries. Eventually, we started filming a reality show for TLC called *17 Kids and Counting*, which was changed to *18 Kids and Counting* and then *19 Kids and Counting* as our family grew. Five of my siblings took their first breaths on television. That makes them, like Truman Burbank, reality TV stars at birth. The show aired on TLC for seven years, and then from 2015 through September 2020, TLC aired a spin-off show about my siblings and me called *Counting On*.

Life on TV has its perks as well as its challenges. For me, one of those challenges has been dealing with other people's expectations. When strangers expect me to make certain decisions—even rooting for me to make them as if I'm a character on a sitcom—they seem to forget that I'm a real person with my own feelings and emotions. Add my family's values to the equation and you get even more criticism, opinions, and debates about how I should live. Every decision is put under a microscope, dissected, and either criticized or praised.

Another challenge has been dealing with the lack of privacy. Whether I'm being recognized in public or chased by photographers, I'm still learning to navigate a life lived publicly.

It hasn't always been easy knowing that millions of strangers have strong opinions about what I should or shouldn't do, say, or be. I am a people pleaser. I don't like conflict. And I don't want to be the center of attention. But that last part comes with being on television—as I quickly learned after my family's show started and a few of my on-air, offhand comments started a movement.

## FREEDOM FROM RULES?

In 2005, a website called Television Without Pity started an online forum about my family. It wasn't especially flattering. (I know; it's hard to believe an online discussion could be critical!) After *14 Children and Pregnant Again* aired, reviews of the documentary poured in. At first, people were just talking about the show—what they liked and didn't like. Then they started talking about my family. Pretty soon, people who had seen the documentary, and perhaps a few who hadn't, were discussing conservative Christianity, home-schooling, courtship, and other topics that were part of my family's fabric. I guess these conversations were a bit afield from the purpose of the Television Without Pity thread, so the forum migrated to a new discussion board that the moderators decided—for reasons I still find amusing—to call Free Jinger. Why in the world did they name it after me? Well, I have a theory.

During several episodes of *19 Kids and Counting*, our family traveled to cities like New York, Chicago, and London. We even went to Disneyland in Southern California. I especially enjoyed those trips because I've always loved big cities. I'll never forget my first visit to Times Square. I loved all the people out and about. The hustle and bustle. It was energizing. Exhilarating. It made me feel small and important at the same time.

My sister Jessa and I liked to pretend we were big-city locals. We would pack for our siblings before trips to New York for filming with *Good Morning America* or the *TODAY* show. We'd try to select the most stylish outfits from the family closet. One time we even met former president Bill Clinton on the *TODAY* set. The producers thought it was neat that he, like us, was from Arkansas. They piled our whole family on this couch and asked the president to take a picture. As Bill Clinton walked toward all of us, he tripped on a cord and accidentally grabbed one of my sisters by the hair to stop his fall. We had a good laugh about it. To me, this perfectly encapsulated the magic of New York. Big cities always held the possibility of a surprise introduction or unexpected encounter.

On one of the talk shows, I mentioned my love for cities, and from what I can tell, that is why I became the namesake of the new Duggar family forum. Critics of the show—and of my family's lifestyle—interpreted my love for cities as a rejection of rural, small-town life. They assumed that if I wanted to live in a big city, that also meant I wanted to break away from the values of my childhood, since most cities are overwhelmingly secular.

Deeply religious and conservative people often talk about the temptations and dangers of big cities. Those who embrace city life typically aim to reinvent themselves or find themselves. Apparently, the moderators of this forum thought I was after the same thing. They thought I had an independent, freedom-loving streak. Their website says they chose the name because they saw in me a spark and spunk.[1] (Also, I think they thought my name was funny. So there's that.)

I admit I'm a little bit touched that the curators of this website named it after me. Not because I appreciate the notoriety but because these people, in their own way, have expressed compassion for me. They think complete freedom is the ticket to happiness.

Yes, I have always wanted to live in a big city. I love living in Los Angeles today—but not for the reasons the Free Jinger founders assumed. I love the excitement. I love the variety of people and the seemingly endless number of places to go and things to do. I don't see the city as a place to find myself or shake free from the world in which I grew up. It doesn't offer me limitless freedom. Instead, living in the city is an opportunity for me to serve others and maximize the life God has given me.

No rules.

No limitations.

No authority beyond yourself.

The curators of the website saw in me a girl they assumed didn't have the good life because she didn't have unbridled freedom.

They thought, *If this girl could break free from her family's ultra-conservative rules—if she could wear what she wanted, date who she wanted, pursue the career she wanted, and eat and drink what she wanted—then she would be happy.*

And they're not alone. Most people think they have to be free from all restraints to be happy. Freedom is the water in which our culture swims, something as essential to most people as gravity. So I think it's caring that others want this for me, even if I don't embrace their version of the "good life."

## FREEDOM FROM RELIGION?

I am not in search of total freedom from rules and biblical morals, but that doesn't mean I am the same Jinger I was when the website started. My faith has changed dramatically. I do not believe the same things I used to believe five or ten years ago about God, the Bible, and the Christian life. I'd like to talk about what has changed. But first, I need to make something clear: I am not deconstructing my faith. *Deconstruction* is a popular word in Christian circles today. It represents a movement of young people who grew up in Christian homes but in adulthood have decided that much, if not all, of what they were taught as children is not for them. They've abandoned their religious beliefs. They tore them down and never rebuilt any kind of faith. Perhaps the most famous example of this is Joshua Harris.

Growing up, I believed a lot of the same things Harris did. I never read *I Kissed Dating Goodbye*, but from what I knew of the book, I was sure its principles worked. It was easy to admire Harris.

Throughout the late '90s and early 2000s, Joshua Harris was one of the country's best-known evangelicals. *I Kissed Dating*

*Goodbye* sold more than a million copies and shaped how an entire generation of Christians, including me, talked about dating, courtship, and relationships. Purity culture was a hot topic, mostly because of Harris. There weren't any young evangelicals with a brighter future.

That's why I was shocked when, in the fall of 2019, this influential author, conference speaker, and former pastor announced that he was no longer a Christian.[2] This announcement came shortly after he and his wife separated (the woman he describes meeting and courting in *Boy Meets Girl*, his follow-up to *I Kissed Dating Goodbye*) and four years after Harris left Covenant Life Church in Gaithersburg, Maryland, where he'd served as a pastor for eleven years. Harris's decisions to leave the ministry, end his marriage, and reject the faith discouraged many Christians. If someone with Harris's pedigree of personal discipleship and ministry preparation could abandon Christianity, it seemed any believer could do the same.

Two years after Harris's surprise announcement, I heard he was selling an online course called "Reframe Your Story," which included a "Deconstruction Starter Pack." It cost $275 (although it was free for anyone who claimed they were hurt by his previous ministry). He said the curriculum was created "for people who are unpacking and have questions and [are] changing their belief who feel really alone in doing that." He also said he "wanted to create something to help people reframe their thinking and to be able to decide for themselves what things they want to hold onto and if they want, to let go of certain religious ideas."[3] Harris's evolution was complete. He was no longer one of the country's most popular Christians. He was now leading something entirely different: the deconstruction movement.

# DECONSTRUCTION OR DISENTANGLEMENT?

In some ways, I think Harris and I found ourselves in a similar place a few years ago. Like him, I grew up in a conservative Christian home. Like him, I was in the public eye from a young age. And like him, I came to a point in adulthood when I realized that my understanding of Christianity was insufficient. But today, there is a massive gulf between Harris and me. Instead of deconstruction, my faith journey is one of disentanglement.

I've come to understand that in the Christianity of my childhood, elements of the true gospel of Jesus Christ were tangled up with false teaching. I've spent eight years unthreading my faith: separating truth from error. Understanding my story of unthreading starts with the fishbowl I grew up in and the two very different expectations that were placed on me as a part of that world.

We've already discussed one of the expectations: that I would find "freedom" and the "good life" by rejecting all rules, commitments, family ties, and religious convictions, much like Joshua Harris and others in the deconstruction movement. But along my journey of disentanglement, I've come to see that unfettered freedom does not produce the good life. In the end, it often leads to more bondage. Why? Because it puts me in charge of my life, and I am not the best judge of what is best for me. If given limitless options and the responsibility of figuring out what is going to make me truly happy, I struggle to commit to anything. I have the same problem when I'm trying to pick a show on Netflix; I just keep scrolling, always wondering if there's a better show out there. In the case of life's big decisions, the question becomes: Is there a better job, home, or relationship? I'm left to constantly second-guess my choices.

However, the opposite of total freedom—man-made rules—is

also a false version of the good life. And others' belief that I should obey these rules was the second expectation I had to wrestle with.

## FREEDOM THROUGH OBEDIENCE?

Not long after the Free Jinger website began, my family went to visit a prominent Christian leader. When asked about my family's response to critics, I mentioned the Free Jinger website, explaining how many people online were saying that I would never be truly free unless I broke away from the strict conservative values I had been raised with. I later journaled about the Christian leader's response, writing:

> He mentioned that he had several people who had done the same to them. Then he slipped away and, little did I know, made a call to one of his staff members and told them to find the nicest shirt and have it printed with writing which says, "Jinger is Free Indeed."

He sent me two of those shirts. One was red with neon-green letters. I still have it.

Why did that prominent Christian leader say I was already free when, at that time, nearly everything about my life was decided for me? I was fourteen years old and didn't have the freedom to choose where I went, what I wore, what music I listened to, or who my friends were. Granted, most teenagers don't have unlimited freedom, but many can agree I had less than most. Obviously, this leader's understanding of freedom was very different from the people in the Free Jinger movement. He believed I was free *because* of the rules, and I understood this perspective.

To-do lists give life structure. They are like guardrails for the day. They identify exactly what needs to be done, and they make it easy to track your progress so you can be sure you are accomplishing your goals. There's something freeing about to-do lists, especially that moment when you cross off a completed item. Man-made religious rules can give the same sense of satisfaction. They are intended to provide tangible proof that life is being lived the way God intended. And there is nothing more freeing than confidence that your decisions are right and you are making God happy.

That's how I understood this leader's definition of freedom. He seemed to be saying that I was already free because I was already following all the rules. There's truth there. The question is, who was I obeying?

You won't find man-made rules in the Bible. God's Word calls for men and women to dress modestly, but it doesn't specify which outfit to pick in the morning. It certainly doesn't say that skirts are more appropriate than jeans! Scripture says our music should honor God, but it doesn't say some genres are better than others. Christians should be sexually pure, but the Word of God doesn't say anything about the specifics of dating. The word *dating* isn't even in the Bible!

Often, these rules have good intentions. They are ways that many sincere Christians try to apply biblical principles. But there's a problem with this vision of freedom: it's based entirely on the individual—on my actions and attitudes. That kind of self-dependence may feel good for a while, but in the end, it's going to crush the soul. I can't obey enough man-made rules to be truly free from the weight of my imperfections. No matter how many restrictions I place on my behavior, my wardrobe, my time, or my appetites, I'll never get away from my sinful self. The Bible says it is not what enters the mouth that defiles the man but what proceeds out of the mouth

(Matthew 15:16–20). In other words, I am messed up because of sin, and no amount of good behavior is going to fix that. I need freedom from myself, not freedom from the world around me.

## WHAT IS TRUE FREEDOM?

I've come to understand that the Free Jinger movement and the conception of freedom behind the "Jinger Is Free Indeed" T-shirt are both wrong. Freedom is not unlimited options. And it's not obedience to man-made rules. So what is it? I'm excited to answer that question in the coming pages.

As I mentioned earlier, my story is one of disentanglement. Of course, this is a story that nearly every true believer could tell. Many of us have realized that our faith was insufficient, incomplete, or inaccurate. When these realizations come, some choose to deconstruct their faith while others refuse to acknowledge their quandary. Perhaps they don't want to admit they might have been wrong, or maybe they are afraid of losing relationships. Neither of those paths was an option for me. I know that Jesus is real and true. This left me not with wanting to deconstruct my faith or ignore the problems but instead choosing to look deeper into the Word of God.

My path involved tracing the threads of true Christianity away from the false version taught by one man—the leader of a strict, conservative version of Christianity that greatly influenced my life. In recent years, I've come to see that the religious system this man built was not reflective of the gracious gospel of Jesus Christ. This man and his teaching produced a lot of legalism in my life.

Thankfully, this false teaching was not the end of my story. God's grace is far more abundant than I realized. It redeemed me, and it can redeem all who have lived, as the apostle Paul said, "in the futility of their minds" (Ephesians 4:17). The grace of God is helping me understand that "if the Son sets you free, you will be free indeed" (John 8:36). In many ways, that verse describes my path from legalism to true freedom. And the beginning of that journey goes back to the fishbowl, to the year 2008, when I was fourteen years old and my private diary was listed on eBay for the absurd amount of $100,000.

# CHAPTER 2

# A Zeal for God

*For most teenage* girls, seeing their private diary for sale on eBay would be their worst possible nightmare. Secret thoughts about boys, parents, and siblings all available for the world to see. Honestly, what could be worse for a girl trying to figure out who she is, what she is passionate about, and what she believes? Thankfully, when I faced that exact scenario at the tender age of fourteen, there was hardly anything shocking for the thief to turn into a profit. Perhaps that's why the person who stole my journal during a visit to our home returned it a few weeks later.

I still have the journal. From time to time, I leaf through the colorful paper and adolescent handwriting and see glimpses of how self-conscious I once was. I mostly used the journal to record what I did each day. These entries include bullet-pointed lists of visitors to our home, tasks accomplished, and friends seen. When I read it today, I'm struck by what is missing. I was afraid to say the wrong thing—to confess my inner desires even in a diary. I didn't express any of the feelings and fears that were a constant part of my childhood. Rather than serving as a true chronicle of Jinger Duggar's inner life, my diary was yet another place of performance: a tool where I practiced projecting the version of myself that I wanted everyone—parents, siblings, friends, fans of the show—to see.

What I was hiding from my journal, from fans of the show, and often from my loved ones wasn't a dark, rebellious spirit. I never dreamed of leaving my family. I genuinely loved my parents and siblings. My parents are kind, loving, and gracious, and they made a happy home for us kids. From spontaneous family bike rides to games of kickball in the backyard to RV trips across the country, they sought to invest in us and be present in our lives. Mine was a sweet childhood.

No, I wasn't longing for a different life. I loved my life. What I was hiding from the world was my fear.

## BECOMING FILLED WITH FEAR

If there's one word—one emotion—that best describes my younger self, it's *fear*. My earliest memory is a moment of sheer terror. I was five years old. My family was living in Little Rock, the capital of Arkansas. My dad, Jim Bob, was part of the state legislature. One day while my dad was at the capitol building, a tornado touched down close to our house. My mom, Michelle, ushered my siblings and me into the bathroom; there must have been eleven children at the time. A bunch of us huddled in the bathtub. I'll never forget my overwhelming anxiety as I stared out the window, convinced the tornado was about to destroy our house and my family. Thankfully, the storm passed, but the fear stayed for years. Thunder terrified me. If I heard it, I'd cry, my body would shake, and I'd panic, thinking another tornado was heading right for us. If a storm came at night, I'd wake my parents, occasionally ending up on a cot in their bedroom.

As I grew older, my fears grew in number. I began to worry that someone in my family would get cancer or some other horrible disease, and I'd have to watch my loved one die. I feared car crashes on the road and snakes in the woods. But by the time I was fourteen, my worst, most all-consuming fear was the fear of what others thought of me.

I don't remember exactly when a desire to please others started to dominate my thinking and decision-making. Perhaps it was when the cameras arrived—I was ten years old at the time—and I realized that millions of people were watching how I lived my life. Or perhaps I was always going to care about the opinions of others and want to hide my imperfections. I am a people pleaser who has always preferred to go with the flow than to share my opinions or make demands.

For years, I thought the best way to please others was to hide my imperfections. This led to some harmful behaviors, including the eating disorder I developed early in my teenage years. Convinced my body was an embarrassment, I ate very little. I'd go days hardly consuming any calories. My weight dropped, but my body image didn't improve. It almost never does in those situations because the weight isn't the problem. No matter how thin I was, I wasn't satisfied with the way I looked. This obsession with body image was terrible for my physical health and it certainly wasn't good for me spiritually. It was a downward spiral that could have gotten worse and worse.

Thankfully, my eating struggles were short-lived, in large part due to my mom's help. She listened to me. She asked me to text her what I was eating and how often. She also monitored my work-out schedule and even turned this into an opportunity to keep her accountable with working out. It was a great way for us to be part-ners in taking care of our health.

Then, at the end of any given day, we'd talk about our days. She encouraged me to make wise choices and get the right number of calories to sustain my body and thrive. I didn't feel judged at all. My mom had shared with me what she's shared with the world: she had struggled with her eating, too, when she was my age. I felt no judgment from her, just love and care. I knew I was going to be okay because she had been through it. It helped me to know that I could eat sufficient calories in a healthy way—grilled chicken, rice, salad, vegetables. Mom gave me the confidence to know I don't have to avoid food to be pretty.

I struggled with self-image because I feared people. I was terrified of the weather and sickness because I feared death. And at the foundation of these fears was a truth about my identity: I did not love God.

## FINDING MY FAITH

As a teenager, I would have called myself a Christian, and nearly everyone around me called themselves Christians too. I was sure that God existed. To me, He was as real as my family. And I knew that God was more than just the being who created everything; He was also in charge of the world and actively upholding the universe "by the word of his power" (Hebrews 1:3). He not only created the world and sustained it but also guided my life—as described in Psalm 139:

> For you formed my inward parts;
> you knitted me together in my mother's womb.
> I praise you, for I am fearfully and wonderfully made.
> Wonderful are your works;
> my soul knows it very well.
> My frame was not hidden from you,
> when I was being made in secret,
> intricately woven in the depths of the earth.
> Your eyes saw my unformed substance;
> in your book were written, every one of them,
> the days that were formed for me,
> when as yet there was none of them. (vv. 13–16)

I'd always given thanks to God for His kindnesses to me. And I assumed that my rank in the Duggar family tree—sixth—my brunette hair, and my personality were gifts from God. But before I was fourteen years old, there was a major problem with my Christian identity.

Hebrews 11:6 says, "Without faith it is impossible to please him, for whoever would draw near to God must believe that he exists and that he rewards those who seek him." I had the first part down: I believed God existed. But the second part—seeking Him? I wasn't doing that. Sure, I recited the prayer of salvation when I was younger. But I didn't really understand repentance. In other words, I wasn't truly sorry when I dishonored and disobeyed God. From time to time I felt bad about my sin or worried about what my parents would think of me, but I cared more about my own happiness than the glory of God.

By God's grace, that changed when I was fourteen. I remember feeling terrified that I didn't truly love Jesus. So I went and found my mom and asked if we could talk. Of course, she said yes. We went into a little prayer closet in our home. I remember crying and telling her that I didn't believe I genuinely loved God. I knew a lot about how to act, things to do and not to do, but none of it was driven by a love for God. It was more about a desire to perform, look good in front of others, and follow the status quo.

I was tired of living this way—trying to be a Christian without God's help. It was draining, and I was exhausted; my religious tank was empty. I realized that I had been wrestling with these feelings for about a year but was just too embarrassed to tell anyone. I was consumed with worry about what they would think of me. They saw me as a Christian. A "good kid." My pride did not want to let me admit that I had been putting on a hypocritical show. But I couldn't stand to exist in that hypocrisy anymore.

I confessed this to my mom and started to cry. I wanted to really know God. I wanted to love and worship Him and enjoy a relationship with Him for the first time. I don't remember what she said to me, but I know I cried out to God and asked Him to save me from my sin.

I had been living for myself, not for God. But that day, a real change happened in my heart. I became committed to living my life to honor God. This change didn't happen because I prayed a certain prayer with the exact right words. I was simply tired of being a performance artist, a religious playactor, a hypocrite. I wanted the real thing. I wanted a relationship with God. Because pleasing Him was now my top priority, the fear of others no longer consumed me.

I'm still prone to people-pleasing. But making others happy no longer dominates my thinking. In the same way, when I became a true Christian, I didn't fear death as much. I knew that when I died, I was going to heaven. Of course, I still didn't want to get in a car wreck, contract a fatal disease, or encounter a tornado, but I knew in my heart that if anything like that happened, I would be in the presence of God.

## FEARING MY NEW FAITH

Despite all this progress, I still struggled with fear. The subject changed, but the intensity remained the same. Specifically, I was afraid that I wasn't obeying and honoring God adequately. I constantly wondered if God was displeased with me. I wanted His approval more than anything but really didn't know what it looked like to have a relationship with Him. I wanted to be close to God but was confused about how exactly to get there.

So much of my uncertainty was because I didn't understand God's character. Instead of thinking of Him as a kind Creator who wanted me to obey Him for my own good and His glory, I primarily thought of God as stern and harsh. I had this idea that He would be disappointed, even angry, if I didn't do exactly what He wanted me to do. Even if I didn't know what He wanted from me in a situation, I thought I could get in trouble for making the wrong choice.

For instance, throughout my teenage years, one of my family's favorite pastimes was broomball—a game similar to hockey that is played on an ice rink while wearing shoes, not skates. We would play several times a week. I especially enjoyed the game and looked forward to the time with my family. But after the chat with my mom, I started to fear that God didn't want me to play. I thought He might instead want me to read my Bible, pray, or do something for others, like help my mom around the house. I didn't think there was anything inherently wrong with broomball. It wasn't a sin for my siblings to play. But I couldn't shake the feeling that broomball wasn't the best use of my time in God's eyes. I even began to fear that if I did go play and that wasn't what God wanted me to do, He would punish me by causing my family to get in a car wreck on the way to the ice rink.

Soon, this uncertainty came with nearly every invitation to do something enjoyable. If it was fun, and I had to decide whether to participate, then I'd second-guess myself, thinking I should instead choose a spiritual activity. I'll never forget the uncertainty I felt when Grandma Duggar would invite me to go shopping, my siblings would ask me to go somewhere, or I'd have free time and want to use it to exercise or relax.

I didn't know then that I was experiencing an overactive conscience. In fact, if you had told me that this was an issue with my conscience, I would have had no idea what you were talking about. I didn't really understand what the conscience was at the time. I mean, I knew I had one, but I didn't quite understand its purpose.

My pastor provides this helpful definition of *conscience*:

> The conscience entreats you to do what you believe is right and restrains you from doing what you believe is wrong. But don't equate the conscience with the voice of God or the law of God. It is a *human* faculty that judges your actions and thoughts by the light of the highest standard you perceive. When you violate your conscience, it condemns you, triggering feelings of shame, anguish, regret, consternation, anxiety, disgrace, and even fear. Conversely, when you follow your conscience, it commends you, bringing joy, serenity, self-respect, well-being, and gladness.[1]

When I was feeling guilty about broomball, that was not God speaking to me. That was my conscience. I didn't know I was training my conscience to tell me that anytime I decided to play a game instead of reading my Bible, I was disobeying God. Of course, the problem wasn't that I had a conscience. It's a gift from the Lord that we should thank Him for. The problem was that my conscience was too active. I trained it to feel guilty for decisions that the Bible didn't condemn. In some cases, things that the Bible encourages—such as exercise or spending time with family—would violate my conscience. I remember multiple times when my family watched a fun movie together while I was upstairs reading my Bible, thinking that's what I should be doing instead.

Mornings could be particularly stressful. I'd wake up and immediately start thinking about what I could do that day to best please God. Often, fasting was one of the first things that came to mind. The Bible talks about fasting as an acceptable spiritual practice, but it never commands believers to fast. Yet if I felt convicted about fasting, I would tell myself I couldn't have food that day. I convinced myself that if I ate, God would not be pleased with me. This was different from the struggle I had with food a few years earlier. Back then, I was worried about what people thought of me. I avoided food because I wanted to appear thin. My concerns with fasting were because I was worried about what God thought of me. My previous struggles with food didn't cross my mind when I tried to figure out if I should fast or not, but it did cross my parents' minds. For that reason, they encouraged me to eat. In fact, my parents directly told me not to fast at that time.

So much of my fear and anxiety after I became a Christian was tied to my overactive conscience. I had created false standards of righteousness: standards that were impossible for me, or anyone, to measure up to. But where did those false standards come from? At the time, I thought my convictions came from the Bible. Now I know that wasn't the case. Now I know that instead of coming from the perfect Word of God, they came from the mind of an imperfect man.

## FOLLOWING BILL GOTHARD

For as long as I can remember, I followed the teachings of a man named Bill Gothard. My parents introduced me and my siblings to Gothard and his seminars. They started listening to his teachings not long after they were married. And they applied many of his principles as they raised me and my siblings. It's no exaggeration to say that Gothard was the most important influence in my life outside of my family. There wasn't a time when I didn't know who he was and admire him. In my diary that was stolen and listed on eBay, I said I couldn't wait to go to one of his conferences for the first time. I remember someone telling me they thought Bill Gothard might be a prophet—a modern-day Elijah sent by God to show Christians how to obey God's Word.

So who exactly is this spiritual leader?

Bill Gothard was raised by Christian parents, and he committed to full-time ministry at age fifteen. He attended Wheaton College, where he received two degrees. When he was a student, he started working with Chicago's inner-city youth. He continued to do that until Wheaton College asked him to come back and teach a course on youth ministry.[2] The curriculum he designed for that class became the Basic Seminar for the Institute in Basic Life Principles (IBLP).[3] In the late 1960s, Gothard started teaching his seminars at churches, Christian schools, camps, and youth programs around the country.[4] His timing could not have been better.

Throughout the 1960s, America's sexual revolution had changed the way many people thought about religion and morality. Millions of Americans stopped saving sex for marriage. Divorce became more common. Drug use skyrocketed. Young people embraced rock and roll, and they used this music to express their independence and live a self-absorbed lifestyle. On top of all that, Americans were dealing with racial tensions, the war in Vietnam, and the threat of nuclear war with the Soviet Union.

For Bible-believing Christians, this was a scary, uncertain time. Parents feared losing their children to sex, drugs, and rock and roll. Bill Gothard offered parents confidence. In his lectures, he claimed he had discovered the key to a successful Christian life. According to Gothard, to enjoy God's blessing, a Christian should closely follow the seven principles he laid out in his seminars: the principles of design, authority, responsibility, suffering, ownership, freedom, and success.

These are universal. They are nonoptional. Every single person in the world must build his or her life around these seven principles. . . . If we don't build our lives around these seven principles, then we're gonna have these root problems. We'll have surface wrong attitudes and surface problems, and our life will be one continuous failure from what God knows our potential could be.[5]

In later chapters, I'll talk in more detail about these principles—and how they dominated my life—but for now, I want to talk about why these principles were effective. First, they were absolute. Gothard spoke in black-and-white terms. He said there was a right way and a wrong way to live. For those who lived the "right" way—who followed his principles—God's blessings were guaranteed. Health, money, success, and happiness were available to them.

Second, his principles were practical. They could be applied immediately. Someone could leave Gothard's seminars with a dozen ways to change his or her life. None of his ideas were presented as theoretical. Even when Gothard claimed what he was saying was based on the Bible, he always stressed practical applications. He often urged people to make a vow after one of his seminars that they would immediately apply what they'd learned.

Finally, these principles were specific. Gothard would teach a principle and then tell you exactly what that principle looked like in everyday life. For instance, when discussing the topic of modesty—which fell under the principle of responsibility, among others—he identified which outfits were modest and which were not. (Long skirts were, which is why my sisters and I wore them all the time—even when we were sleeping or swimming.) That may seem too strict for many, but for millions of Americans, it was comforting and liberating.

These rules were clear and easy to follow. And according to Gothard, following his principles was the same as obeying God. For the nervous Christian parent, these principles were the perfect cure to the moral chaos of the 1960s and '70s. A few years after he started teaching his principles across the country, Gothard was filling stadiums. He was an evangelical celebrity.

## REAPING WHAT I'D SOWN

By the time I was born in 1993, an entire Christian subculture had formed around Gothard's teaching. I was born into that subculture. The certainty of his teachings—the guarantees he promised—attracted many Christian parents in the 1960s, '70s, and '80s, including mine. He talked a lot about reaping what you sow. The idea was that if you planted the right lifestyle—in other words, made choices that aligned with his teachings—then God would bless your life and you would reap the lifestyle you had sowed. That method of success gave thousands a sense of control as the world around them seemed to be falling apart.

Here's an example of this teaching from Gothard:

Life is hooked up in a very delicate cause-and-effect sequence. . . . Here's a man who wonders why he's having business problems, financial problems. He doesn't know that God has a clear relationship between his moral life and his business life. Now there are other relations, too, that would affect business, but that's just one. Here's a person who wonders why his children are reacting. He doesn't know that God has a very clear relationship between his honoring of his parents and the response of his children to him.

And in more and more ways, God has a very clear cause-and-effect sequence.[6]

That lesson was both comforting and terrifying to me. It was comforting because it turned life into a series of deposits and withdrawals. All I had to do was deposit the exact lifestyle Gothard advocated, and I would withdraw health, money, a wonderful husband, and a bushel of godly kids. But this cause-and-effect view was also terrifying because I thought I would experience devastating consequences for any mistakes I made.

For years, I was convinced that Bill Gothard was the finest Bible teacher in America and that his so-called secrets to success were the path to personal fulfillment.[7] Through those years, I had a self-righteous attitude. I pitied those who didn't follow these principles. I thought their ignorance would lead to a life of spiritual darkness. They'd miss out on God's blessings and protection because they didn't know these principles.

When millions of people watched me on television during my teenage years, they saw a girl who was putting these principles into action in every area of her life. She was committed. She was convinced that she had found the secret to success.

I certainly had a unique childhood. But my spiritual journey is not that different from anyone else's. Many were also influenced by Bill Gothard's teachings. Others have had someone tell them that a certain teaching came from God when it really just came from man. And others have been pressured to follow a set of extra rules, in addition to the commands in Scripture, in order to be acceptable to God. In that circumstance, the question they eventually face is the same one I faced: *How do I know whether what I believe is consistent with the Word of God or is a false religious system invented by man?* There are often elements of truth mixed in with false teaching. There are good ideas that help to honor God tangled with bad ideas that cause a lot of heartache. How do you know the difference? How do you disentangle truth from error?

For me, the disentanglement process began with understanding what the Bible actually says and comparing it to what Gothard said. Did they match up? Finding the answer required a closer look at Gothard's seven basic life principles—the same principles I'd been applying in front of a reality TV audience throughout my childhood.

# CHAPTER 3

# The Principles

*Not long ago,* a friend asked me how many siblings my husband, Jeremy, has. I said, "Two," and, without thinking, added, "so he grew up in a small family." My friend laughed and said, "Three kids isn't what I'd call a small family." Of course, she's right. I'd guess the typical American family has about two kids, so three is above average. But when you grow up in a family with nineteen children, three can seem like an empty house.

That conversation was another reminder of how different my childhood was from the typical American. The size of my family was a big reason (no pun intended) that my life was unique. Hardly anyone can say they have eighteen siblings, all of whose names start with the letter *J.* Of the handful of families that large, I can think of only ours and one other—the Bates family—that had camera crews following them around, filming people who didn't watch television.

Beyond the cameras and the size of my family, the way we dressed was different. How we talked to one another was unique, and not just because we had Arkansas accents. I hardly fought with my siblings, which is pretty wild considering the number of us, and we shared clothes, shoes, and curling irons. I also didn't have a typical education. I was homeschooled and didn't go to college.

As a teenager, I knew my life was different from most girls my age. I also knew that a lot of people had strong opinions about what my future should look like. But I didn't think I needed the criticism or advice, no matter how well-intentioned. I knew exactly why God had put me on earth. The future was so clear, I could see it in my head and trace every major event in my life. I was going to marry in my early twenties (if not by the time I was eighteen or nineteen). I was sure I'd marry a godly, Christian man who worked hard, loved children, and made me laugh. I would quickly become a mother and have as many kids as possible. I'd stay home and take care of our growing family while my husband worked to keep us out of debt.

I was not only certain I'd be a mother but also confident about how I'd parent my kids. I'd teach them to respect my husband and me. They would rarely argue, and they wouldn't rebel because I was going to teach them the same basic life principles that had guided me. I tended to judge parents if I saw their older children acting up. I'd think, *If they only knew what I know about parenting, their kid wouldn't behave that way.*

I was convinced that after marrying at a young age, my husband and I would be madly in love for decades. Sure, we might have a disagreement or two, but in general, there'd be unity. He would lead, the children and I would gladly submit to him, and our family would enjoy peace, success, and health. Other families would look at us as a model of what God can do for a family if they obey His principles.

## MY EXPECTATIONS FOR THE FUTURE

By the time I was having these teenage conceptions, my older brother was already a father. Many of my sisters gladly volunteered to watch our nieces and nephews. They also offered to babysit for family friends. I joined them from time to time, but I wasn't passionate about kids. I wasn't the girl who begged to hold other people's babies. I admire those who strongly desire to have a lot of children. But these days I just can't say I feel the same way. Of course, I adore my two precious daughters. Being their mom is one of the greatest joys of my life. I love my children with my whole heart and soul. But my current perspective on parenthood and what that looks like for me is very different from the perspective of the culture in which I was raised.

I grew up assuming that a woman starts having children as soon as she is married and continues until she physically can't have any more. Even if she has severe health issues or feels overwhelmed by the number of children she already has, she cannot stop having children. This belief was largely due to Gothard's teaching. His "Basic Care Booklet" says this about pregnancy and children:

> What if another pregnancy will cause health problems? What should a woman do if her doctor tells her that another pregnancy will create serious or even life-threatening complications? What should a man do if he is warned, "If you get your wife pregnant, you will be responsible for her death!"?
>
> In answering these questions, the following factors must be carefully evaluated:
>
> 1. God has ultimate control.
>
> If God wants to give a child to a couple, He is also able to give the level of health in the mother and the child that will bring the greatest glory to Him. . . .
>
> 2. No Decision Should Be Based on Fear
>
> God has not given us a spirit of fear. Therefore, fear is from Satan and not from God.[1]

Gothard also said Christian families should ignore potentially life-saving medical advice because "all births require sacrifice on the part of the parents" and "many predictions do not come true."[2] He taught that God's will was for a woman to have children no matter what, even if her life was in danger.

In Genesis 1, God told Adam and Eve to "be fruitful and multiply and fill the earth and subdue it" (v. 28).

Gothard used this verse and others similar to teach that Christian families not only should have as many children as possible but also were sinning against God if they didn't. This is what Jim Sammons, a teacher with IBLP, said during a lecture about finances:

> You know, I used to wonder, God, why don't you stop abortion in our country? [My wife] and I have been actively involved in the right to life movement, and I sit as an advisor on a board of a pregnancy crisis center, and I work with legislators trying to get them to change the law and it just doesn't seem to be working. I used to wonder, God, why aren't you doing it? Proverbs 21:1 says, "The heart of the king is in the hand of the Lord" [v. 1 DRA]—you can turn it whatever way you want! Cause the king, the judges, the congressmen, to change. And then it was like God said, "That law, Jim, reflects your view and the view of Christians, of my people." And I personally don't believe God will ever let that law change until God's people change their view on children.[3]

I interpreted this to mean that if a husband and wife used any kind of birth control for family planning, they were as good as aborting their children. Sammons went on to suggest that such couples were guilty not only of abortion but also of rejecting Jesus. He said:

> There was one verse that was interesting—it was Matthew 18:5, and Jesus says, "And whoso shall receive one such little child in My name, receiveth Me" [KJ21]. And I decided to look up the word

*receive* in Thayer's Greek-English Lexicon of the New Testament, and I was amazed when I saw there it means *to receive into one's family in order to bring up and to educate.* And Jesus said, if you receive that child, it's like receiving me. I realized that it was like by rejecting children, we had rejected our Lord.[4]

Even though Jesus was not talking about families giving birth to children in the passage from Matthew 18, Sammons used it to tell thousands of wives and mothers to have as many children as possible. To refuse would be to reject Jesus Himself. You can imagine the guilt this placed on many women—including me.

This teaching was a misrepresentation of what the Bible says. Are children a gift from God? Absolutely—an incredible one! I cannot imagine my life without Felicity and Evangeline, and I thank God for them. Is it a blessing to have children? Without a doubt. Did God command humankind to have children? Yes—it's a basic requirement for civilizations to grow and flourish. But the Bible never tells women how many they should have. Pastor John Piper has something helpful to say about this. He wrote,

> We love those big families, and anybody that wants to can have a big family in this church. It is a good thing, if you bring those kids up to be radical soldiers for Jesus.[5]

But his teaching doesn't stop there. According to Desiring God, a ministry Piper founded:

> Just because something is a gift from the Lord does not mean that it is wrong to be a steward of when or whether you will come into possession of it. It is wrong to reason that since A is good and a gift from the Lord, then we must pursue as much of A as possible.

God has made this a world in which tradeoffs have to be made and we cannot do everything to the fullest extent. . . .

Although it is true that "blessed is the man whose quiver is full of [children]" (Psalm 127:5 NASB), we need to realize that God has not given everyone the same size quiver. And so birth control is a gift from God that may be used for the wise regulation of the size of one's family, as well as a means of seeking to have children at the time which seems to be wisest.[6]

I didn't understand this as a teenager. Based on Gothard's teaching, and the teachings of men like Jim Sammons at IBLP, I assumed that wives should have as many children as physically possible. And that intimidated me. Yet I never thought my feelings could affect the course of my life. So whether I was anxious about it or not, having lots of children was in my future. My purpose was essentially wrapped up in being a wife and mother. Those two roles were the primary reasons God had put me on earth. I didn't question that. Also, I wanted to please God, so if a big family was a primary way to honor Him, then I was willing to get over my fear and have as many children as I could.

Of course, God does call many women to be wives and mothers. Titus 2:4–5 says young women should "love their husbands and children, to be self-controlled, pure, working at home, kind, and submissive to their own husbands." That is a lot of work, but it's an impactful, God-honoring, and fulfilling life. That said, womanhood is not confined to being only a mother. Women, like men, are made in God's image, which means they are made to know and glorify Him. A Christian woman's identity is found in Jesus, not in her roles, which will change throughout her life.

When a woman becomes a Christian, she is God's workmanship. The good works that God prepares won't be the same for everyone.

While a woman can walk in good works as a wife and mom, she can also do that through a vocation, service to the church, and by loving others well. I hope that's something all women know, especially those who are not married or who struggle with infertility.

Women who never marry or have children can absolutely glorify God. I didn't realize that when I was younger. I've had to disentangle the truth of my identity in Christ from a narrow view of my identity as primarily a wife and mother.

## BILL GOTHARD'S BASIC LIFE PRINCIPLES

Nineteen-year-old me had all that confidence because I assumed life is like a recipe book: use the right ingredients in the right way, and the outcome is virtually guaranteed. Ever heard that famous saying from *Forrest Gump* (which I haven't seen—no surprise): "My momma always said, 'Life was like a box of chocolates. You never know what you're gonna get'"?[7] The idea is that life is unpredictable: you take it as it comes. If I'd watched that movie when I was a teenager, I would have thought that was a silly thing to believe. Life was the opposite of a box of chocolates. It was predictable, repeatable, with few surprises. All you needed were the right ingredients—the principles that were key to a successful Christian life. If I followed them, then God would bless me. If I didn't, then God would not bless me. If another woman was struggling—if she didn't get the husband she wanted or children that were a blessing or financial security—it was probably because she didn't know these principles.

Those who watched me on television, particularly when I was a teenager, saw me living out these principles. No doubt they had some questions about the way I lived. Why did I dress that way?

Why did I say that? Why did I go there or do that? Many of the answers can be traced to Gothard's seven basic life principles.

## The Principle of Design

Gothard described his first principle—the principle of design—this way: "God has a precise purpose for each person, object, and relationship that He creates. As we understand and live in harmony with His design, we will discover self-acceptance, identity, and fulfillment in life."[8] I understood this to mean that if I recognized God's design and thanked Him for it, I would find satisfaction and fulfillment.

## The Principle of Authority

According to Gothard's principle of authority, God assigns "various responsibilities to parents, church leaders, government officials, and other authorities." What's more, "as we learn to acknowledge and honor these authorities, we can see God work through them to provide direction and protection in our lives."[9] I believed that in doing so, I would experience inner peace.

## The Principle of Responsibility

Gothard described his third principle—responsibility—as "realizing that I am responsible to God for all my thoughts, words, actions, attitudes, and motives and that I must clear up every past offense against God and others."[10] According to Gothard, this is necessary to achieve a clear conscience.

## The Principle of Suffering

The fourth principle—suffering—is closely related to the third principle of responsibility. For this one, Gothard said Christians should welcome "the chastening of the Lord and the sorrows and hurts of life as necessary for my maturity and future leadership."[11] Often, those "sorrows and hurts of life" are a result of conflict—people saying unkind and untrue things. In response to the suffering this conflict produces, Gothard said believers must forgive others. Based on his teaching, I thought that if I followed this principle, I would experience genuine joy.

## The Principle of Ownership

The fifth basic life principle is ownership, which Gothard described as "knowing that everything I have or will have is entrusted to me by the Lord and is to be used in ways that will benefit the Lord and the lives of others."[12] So if I yielded my rights to God, then I'd enjoy true security.

## The Principle of Freedom

For the sixth principle—freedom—Gothard had a clever description: "Enjoying the desire and the power to do what is right rather than claiming the privilege to do what I want."[13] By embracing this view of freedom, I expected to experience moral purity.

## The Principle of Success

Here's how Gothard defined the seventh and final principle: "The principle of success involves building God's Word into every aspect of our being so we can receive His direction for every decision."[14] Gothard said that if I filled my mind with God's Word, then God would direct my daily decisions. The result? A successful life. He elaborated on this in his seminar. At one point he said that if we follow these principles, we can be sure that we will always succeed.[15] That's what I believed for many, many years. I saw Gothard's principles as the ticket to success. I figured if I followed them, God would make it clear to me what decisions I was supposed to make and not make. He would do that for the big decisions in life, like who I was supposed to marry, and the smallest of events, including questions like "What am I supposed to eat?"

## THE PRINCIPLES IN MY LIFE

Most have probably never heard those principles before, but for me, not a day went by when I didn't apply them to my life in some way. Here are a couple of examples of what that looked like.

### Courtship

Courtship was probably the most famous application of these principles in my life. It was one of the most talked about aspects of the show. When I was younger, I didn't understand why so many people thought it was fascinating, bizarre, or ridiculous. To me, courtship was a normal, healthy way to live out the principles of design and authority.

Courtship is the process through which a young man and woman go from being friends to spouses. Two people don't enter a courtship unless they are considering marriage. Courtship doesn't have to lead to the altar, but there's an expectation that the courting couple is spending time together because they are serious about potentially marrying each other, even if they don't know each other well when the relationship begins.

This process means parents decide if their daughters can get to know a particular man. And the parents also have final say over whether or not the daughter and suitor can get married. It's a little different for sons. It seems like they have more freedom than the girls. Most of the time within this culture, a young man can pursue a girl and decide if he wants to marry her. The parents have input, but they aren't as involved throughout the process. For my sisters and me, this process didn't mean we had no say in who we were going to marry. Rather, it meant that young men who were interested in a relationship with me had to first get my parents' approval. Jeremy and I weren't set up by my mom and dad. We decided for ourselves that we wanted to be in a relationship and consider marriage. But it took more than five months for our relationship to begin because we didn't initially have my parents' approval. They wanted to get to know Jeremy. His background and theology were different from ours, and that gave my parents pause. When they did approve and we began courting, we followed specific guidelines. We didn't go on one-on-one dates. Our time together took place at one of our families' homes, or we had a sibling tag along with us if we went shopping, to a restaurant, or went for a walk. We also didn't hold hands until we were engaged or kiss until marriage. My parents encouraged us to follow these guidelines.

I was committed to those courtship principles. I never thought about going out on a date with a guy by myself or spending time with a guy before he'd gained my parents' approval. I was determined to reserve all of myself for my future husband. If I gave any affection to a guy who didn't become my husband, I thought I'd be giving pieces of my heart to him, which would make it harder for me to give all of myself to my husband when the time came.

I wrote about this a lot in my journal. Here's an example from July 22, 2015:

> We went to the courtship class at church. I was so greatly convicted by the message talking about the dating spirit. I am so guilty in this area. This morning I was thinking about all of the wrongs it seems like I've been getting myself wrapped up in. Saddened and so sick of this state. Asking God for answers.

I saw attraction as being a distraction. I was so afraid of having a "dating spirit" that there were times when I wouldn't even talk to a young man I might've been attracted to. Here's another of my journal entries in which I conflated having thoughts about a guy with being attacked by Satan:

> The past few days I have had a flood of thoughts about a young man. I was wisely encouraged to have a prayer target so when the temptation comes to dwell on such thoughts, I'm going to stop and pray for my sister. It's really cool. What Satan meant for evil, God used for good.

That's how I viewed any thoughts of attraction: as being evil and from Satan. I needed to fight against them, resist them with prayer. Today, I recognize that there were real problems with how I thought about relationships between guys and girls.

I was so afraid of defrauding guys or giving away my heart that I thought it was safer to avoid them altogether. I now see how harmful that view was. In relationships, there's no substitute for spending time—lots of time—with your boyfriend or girlfriend. Getting to know them in their context of life and family, spending hours talking, going on dates, and experiencing all sorts of life situations together is so valuable. Courtship can become so highly controlled by parents, regulated, and overseen that it doesn't allow for this level of openness and vulnerability.

There was a practical problem with courting, and my fear of having a dating spirit, when it came to my relationship with Jeremy. My determination to guard my heart made it difficult for Jeremy to figure out whether I liked him. He would ask Jessa what I was saying about him or if I had any interest. He, of course, assumed that I'd shared these things with my sisters. But I hadn't. I hadn't told

Jessa or any of my other siblings how I felt about Jeremy. I wasn't comfortable revealing my feelings because I was trying to guard my heart.

When Jeremy and I did begin our relationship, we felt a lot of pressure. We didn't know each other well, yet from the moment we started talking on the phone, there was an expectation of marriage. That can be emotionally challenging. I know it was for me. When my dad gave Jeremy and me permission to court, I wasn't yet convinced I wanted to marry him. I loved being around him, I respected him, but I didn't know him well enough to say whether or not I wanted to spend the rest of my life with him. After all, we hadn't had a lot of in-depth conversations. Our courtship sometimes made it tough to have those necessary conversations in an informal setting. When we were with each other in person, we had a chaperone, which a lot of times was one of my younger siblings. We obviously didn't want to have those important discussions that every couple needs to have if a brother or sister was in earshot. Instead of enjoying our time together, we skipped the "friendship" stage and went straight to the "are we going to marry" stage. Looking back, I see how important that friendship stage is because friendship is such an important part of marriage. Despite those challenges, Jeremy and I were still able to grow together and figure out that we did want to marry. Marrying him was one of the best decisions I ever made.

## Modesty

Watch any episode of *19 Kids and Counting* or *Counting On* and you'll probably notice that I only wore skirts. Every skirt had to reach at least below the knee. I also wore blouses and shirts that covered the shoulders. That dress code was a big part of my life because Gothard said modesty was a serious responsibility for every Christian.

The Bible does say modesty is important. First Timothy 2:9 says women are to "adorn themselves in respectable apparel, with modesty and self-control, not with braided hair and gold or pearls or costly attire." But it doesn't say how long skirts should be or mandate shirtsleeves.

Beyond the principle of responsibility, Gothard tied his specific dress code to the principles of authority, design, and freedom. Modesty was an application of authority because I was submitting to what I thought God said about modesty. Dressing modestly was also part of the freedom Gothard defined as "not the right to do what I want, but the power to do what I ought."[16] I had no problem wearing what I thought I ought to. In fact, I wanted to dress conservatively and for everyone around me to do the same. I remember being so disappointed when a friend of mine started wearing pants. I thought that she had stepped away from the truth she knew she should be following. I was heartbroken and prayed for her. I was concerned about where her life was headed.

But most of all, based on Gothard's teaching, I saw it as my responsibility to protect others' moral purity by dressing modestly. If someone struggled with impure thoughts because of something I wore, then I bore some responsibility for that person's sin. I needed to make sure no one stumbled because of my outfit choices. That's why I cared so much about the length of my skirts, even down to the inches.

Now that I have walked away from the Gothard teachings, I find this idea deeply problematic. Though the Bible warns against causing others to sin (Luke 17:1–2), it doesn't say that if someone has impure thoughts about me, I am at fault. That logic shifts blame away from the individual committing the sin. In extreme circumstances, it can put blame on the victims of assault instead of the abusers. This is exactly what Gothard taught. In a document called

"Counseling Sexual Abuse" that was given to attendees at IBLP's Advanced Training Institute, he said God allows victims to be abused because of:

- "immodest dress"
- "indecent exposure"
- "being out from protection of our parents"
- "being with evil friends"[17]

## HOW I'VE DISENTANGLED THE PRINCIPLES

Those are two of the more famous examples of how I lived out these principles. However, I've since realized the need to disentangle the truth from the errors in the way Gothard taught me to apply them.

### Disentangling Design

God made me a specific way. Psalm 139:13–14 says:

> For you formed my inward parts;
> you knitted me together in my mother's womb.
> I praise you, for I am fearfully and wonderfully made.
> Wonderful are your works;
> my soul knows it very well.

God designed everything about me: from my height and eye color to my personality and talents. That's true, and it's beautiful.

God not only made me on purpose but also has a purpose for how I live. All of us owe our existence to God, and He designed us to obey and honor Him. Dozens of verses talk about God's purpose for all people, but the simplest might be 1 Corinthians 10:31, which says, "Whether you eat or drink, or whatever you do, do all to the glory of God."

Gothard had a lot of ideas about design that I no longer believe. For example, he said that one of the best ways to find out God's design, and why He allows defects in our lives, is to look at the sins of our forefathers. Gothard said,

> Teenagers are asking a very profound question. They're saying, "If God is really a God of love, could not He have made children so that the sins of the parents would not in any way affect the children?" God could've made us that way, but He didn't. So it is that the sins of the parents are passed on to the children.[18]

According to Gothard, if someone's grandfather was an alcoholic, it would take "five generations of no liquor at all just to remove the proneness to alcoholism that's passed on to the children."[19] That same principle applied to any sin: anger, laziness, lying, or lust. If my great-grandfather struggled with anger, Gothard said it would be passed on to me. To break this family curse, to reverse the way my family was designed, I had to set up special disciplines and limits. I needed to create barriers to committing those sins or being exposed to them in any way.

Let me explain what this would look like in my life. For a while, I tried to avoid places that even sold alcohol, including restaurants, grocery stores, and convenience stores. I thought this was the best way to avoid the abuse of alcohol, something I was sure would be inevitable if I let myself be exposed to it at all. The same principle— avoiding any association with a potential sin—dominated my life. So much of what I didn't wear, listen to, or eat was not just because I was trying to avoid disobeying God. It was because I was trying to stay away from any possible associating with disobedience. In recent years, I've learned that I am not always more prone to a particular sin because a previous generation struggled with it. I've also learned there's a difference between disobeying God and interacting with someone or something that would not be godly behavior. The two are not the same.

## Disentangling Authority

What I've disentangled in recent years isn't so much Gothard's view of courtship and parents' authority before marriage; there's more than one way to find a spouse. It's what Gothard said about parents' authority *after* marriage that's problematic.

He taught that when a couple gets married, there is a new structure of protection and authority, and the husband is the head of the house. But he also said the young couple is "under counsel of father and father-in-law, mother and mother-in-law."[20] In volume 1 of his *Men's Manual*, he said, "A grandfather's responsibility for his sons and daughters does not end when they finish their education or when they are married. His responsibility continues for as long as he lives!"[21] This idea is nowhere in God's Word. Rather, God's Word commands, "Therefore a man shall leave his father and his mother and hold fast to his wife, and they shall become one flesh" (Genesis 2:24). Gothard invented a system whereby grown children still have to listen to their parents and obey their counsel. He maintained the authority of the parents, even after the marriage vows.

At times, this has played itself out in my marriage in tricky ways, especially in the early years after Jeremy and I became husband and wife. I had always felt like Jeremy and I had to check with my parents, see what they thought about the decisions we were making. I felt this way when we were buying our first house in Texas and when we decided to move to California. I had to remind myself that at the end of the day, we could get advice, but Jeremy and I would make the final decision. We were our own family and we had to make decisions that would honor God and be best for us and our children. Figuring out how to navigate those dynamics was something I had to do as I disentangled what Gothard taught about parental authority from what I believed the Bible truly said.

## Disentangling Responsibility

Gothard taught me that it was my responsibility to clear up all offenses, to make sure I asked God and others to forgive me for every action.

God loves forgiveness. John MacArthur often says, "Never are we more like the God we proclaim than when we forgive."[22] I have seen again and again that we are blessed to be forgiven by God and others. I've also experienced the peace that comes with forgiving those who've offended me. But I've had to disentangle the truth about forgiveness—and my responsibility in that process—from the unhealthy version of it I learned from Gothard.

As a teenager, I used to be terrified that I had some unconfessed sin. I thought that if I hadn't cleared up "every past offense against God and others," as Gothard taught,[23] then God would punish me. Before bed, I'd scan my memory from the day's events and make sure I hadn't offended a sibling, said something disrespectful to my parents, or had a negative thought about a friend or family member. If I thought of some wrong I'd committed, I'd quickly ask God to forgive me and take the first opportunity to ask the person I'd offended to forgive me, too, even if they didn't know I'd offended them.

This uncertainty could be overwhelming on Sunday mornings when our church took Communion. This part of Christian worship is an opportunity to remember what the Lord did for sinners on the cross. It's meant to bring joy to every believer. When

Christians drink the cup and eat the bread, the Bible says they "proclaim the Lord's death until he comes" (1 Corinthians 11:26). Taking Communion is serious, but it's also a celebration. Yet most Sunday mornings, I didn't see it that way. I thought of it more as a game of Russian roulette. I was convinced that if I took Communion with some unconfessed sin I didn't know about, then God would punish me, possibly with death.

Before taking Communion, I'd rack my brain, trying to think of anything I could have said or done that might require an apology or confession. Even if I couldn't think of anything, I still wouldn't take Communion if I thought there might be the smallest possibility I was forgetting a sin.

This is an unhealthy view because it assumes that God wants to punish me—and that it's my responsibility to avoid that punishment. But for the person whose faith is in Jesus, the Bible says the opposite is true. Psalm 103:12 promises, "As far as the east is from the west, so far does [God] remove our transgressions from us."

## Disentangling Suffering

Gothard taught me that if I was suffering, there was a good chance it was because of some hidden or secret sin in my life. I was disobeying God in some way, and that was why I was experiencing pain and hardship. He even said that "most illnesses today are the result of bitterness, or guilt, or just lack of love."[24] I quickly became terrified that if I didn't do everything I could to be agreeable, I'd face the consequences in the form of suffering.

Of course, sin and disobedience can certainly produce a lot of pain. For instance, if someone is angry and they punch a wall and break their hand, their sin has caused them pain. But sometimes suffering happens for reasons unknown to the believer. The Bible says that sometimes the reason for our suffering is to help us grow closer to God. Sometimes it's simply a result of living in a broken world. And yes, sometimes it's because of sin. But, contrary to what Gothard taught, there's not always a way to know why suffering happens.

I firmly disagree with what Gothard said about Job—an Old Testament man who lost his wealth, friends, health, and children. After Job lost everything he loved, three friends visited him. They figured that he must be suffering because he did something wrong. They didn't know what he did wrong, but they assumed that someone suffering as much as Job must have made a mistake. Gothard not only agrees with Job's friends, he at one point said he knows something they don't—why Job was suffering: he was afraid. According to Gothard, Job apparently had three fears: He feared his children would rebel. He feared he would lose his health. He feared that he would lose his possessions. The reason we know that is because in the third chapter, Job gave us something of a confession. He said, "The thing that I greatly feared has come upon me, and the thing that I was greatly afraid of has now happened to me!" (v. 25, paraphrase). No wonder God tells us over and over in Scripture, "Don't fear! Fear not."[25]

If you assume that the story of Job is a warning against fear, you are going to be more afraid. At least that's what happened to me when I was younger! I was afraid that if I felt fear, God would punish me for that.

What Gothard said is simply not true. The Bible tells us why these events happened to Job, and it's not because Job feared those things. It's because God said Job was righteous, and Satan wanted to destroy his faith. But Gothard's teaching paralyzed me with fear. I thought that anything I feared would come to be. I felt like my destiny was fully dependent on me and my mind, as if I were controlling my circumstances by what I thought.

I'll never forget listening to Austin Duncan, the college pastor at my church, teach through the book of Job a few years ago. That series changed how I think about suffering and my own fear. Austin said this:

> I think this is helpful for us because it teaches us that we can't dodge suffering, that you can't manage your life, you can't control your circumstances, you can't exercise enough or plan enough or save enough money or work your way into a place of security . . . to avoid suffering. [26]

This lesson from the book of Job taught me that my suffering is not necessarily a result of my disobedience or some hidden fears in my subconscious. It helped me live out my faith with confidence.

## Disentangling Success

Through Gothard's teachings I became convinced that if I obeyed these principles, if I applied them every day and to every part of my life just as he told me to, I would enjoy extraordinary success. My marriage would be strong, and so would my bank account. Then God would use me to be a blessing to others. Non-Christians, and perhaps some Christians who were struggling with their health, relationships, or finances, would see my success and want the same blessings. That, Gothard said, was the ultimate goal: to be a light to the nations, a witness to the blessings God pours out on those who obey Him. I think that was my family's driving motivation for being on television; we were convinced that if viewers saw the joy and harmony these principles produced in our lives, then they would want to be Christians and live like we did. Our goal was to show the world a positive, compelling view of Christianity.

Just as problematic as Gothard's opinions, however, was his

guarantee of success for everyone who follows his rules. Gothard taught that the future I wanted—husband, kids, financial freedom, and health—would be mine if I followed everything he was teaching. He claimed his seminars were the key to success, and I was sure to get all those blessings if I obeyed. In other words, I was being taught a version of the health and wealth gospel.

The health and wealth gospel is simply this: God wants to give His children money and physical health, but they must have faith that He will bless them. The size of someone's financial success is proportional to the amount of that person's faith and obedience. Here's what Gothard said about money: "God uses riches to bless those who obey his commandments, and he removes money from those who violate his commandments."[27] If I saw a family who was following Gothard's principles and they owned their house outright—had no debt on it—or they could afford to give generously, I assumed God was blessing them because they were so committed to the principles.

Millions of Americans believe the health and wealth gospel. There is no shortage of preachers and televangelists who have gained millions of followers by teaching this version of Christianity. When teachers promise healing for those who have enough faith, tens of thousands show up at their crusades, hoping they have enough faith to leave with a restored body.

When I was a teenager, I would have said that I rejected the health and wealth gospel. Gothard himself would have criticized what prosperity preachers were teaching. But I did believe that obedience was the key to success in life. I was convinced that if I obeyed, God would reward me with the blessings. In other words, I believed the health and wealth gospel. It looked a little different from the popular version that shows up on television and in some of America's biggest churches, but it was essentially the same message.

In recent years, I've started to understand that what I thought was the key to success was actually a recipe for spiritual failure.

## THE EFFECTS OF GOTHARD'S BASIC LIFE PRINCIPLES

Ultimately, Gothard's seven principles produced exhaustion and fear in my life. I was consumed with being introspective, overcome by paranoia. I obsessively dissected my life—my thoughts, words, and actions—because I was terrified that a sin might sneak in and cause me to lose God's blessings. If I forgot to ask forgiveness for a single sin, I felt condemned. I believed that I needed to know everything Gothard taught and that I needed to obey every one of his principles and their associated rules, no matter how obscure. Otherwise, my life would be a failure.

If that was true of all seven principles, it was especially the case for the principle of authority. It seemed like Gothard thought that was the most important one. He seemed to connect the rest of the principles back to authority, as if it was the foundation for everything he taught. Disobey that and I would remove myself from what Gothard called "the umbrella of authority" or "umbrella of protection,"[28] thereby opening myself up to attacks from Satan.

# CHAPTER 4

# Life under the umbrella

*Once upon a* time, a twenty-one-year-old Christian woman met the man of her dreams. He was kind, smart, hardworking, and handsome. Most importantly, he was a committed Christian. He loved God and wanted to obey Him. The couple started spending time together and soon became convinced that the Lord was directing them to marriage. She was overjoyed. Ever since she became a Christian, she had wanted to be a wife and mother. She took her boyfriend to visit her parents—who were not Christians—and the daughter and her boyfriend told them their intentions to marry. After the young man left, the parents told their daughter, "We don't think that you should marry him." The daughter asked why they felt this way. They said, "We can't give you a good reason; we just don't think you ought to marry him."[1]

Bill Gothard presented that fictional scenario at one of his seminars. After hooking his audience with this compelling story, he asked them a question: What should the daughter do? Should she and the young man marry, or should they submit to her parents' wishes even though the mom and dad are not Christians and have no good reason for disliking the young man? Gothard said the latter decision is the right one. He told his audience the parents' authority is absolute, no matter the circumstances and no matter how misguided their decisions. Parents must always be obeyed.

My mother-in-law, Diana, faced nearly that exact scenario almost forty years ago. Jeremy's mother was not raised in a Christian home. Not long after she became a follower of Christ, she met a young pastor named Chuck Vuolo. She liked him and wanted to date him. But her parents had concerns. They were proud of their daughter. She was an accomplished professional violinist. She had traveled internationally, playing in some of the finest orchestras. Her parents thought their daughter's newfound Christianity was a phase. And they were concerned that if she married this pastor, she would be stuck in religion the rest of her life and would have to give up her promising career.

If Diana had followed Bill Gothard's teaching at the time, she likely would have ended the relationship with Chuck because her parents didn't approve. If she had followed the principle of authority, then the life my in-laws built together, their years of ministry, and the three children they brought into this world would have never happened.

Fifteen years ago, if I'd met a girl in the same situation as Diana when she fell in love with Chuck, I probably would have urged her, for her own protection, not to disregard her parents. At the time, I believed all disobedience to parents—no matter the circumstances— was dangerous. I'd fully embraced a concept Gothard called "the umbrella of authority."

## THE UMBRELLA OF AUTHORITY

According to this concept, God gives every person authority figures who must always be obeyed. Just as an umbrella protects against rain, these authorities protect a person from spiritual harm, including suffering, pain, and temptations from Satan. But, also like an umbrella, the protection is limited. During a downpour, one wrong step (or strong gust of wind) could leave an individual soaked. Likewise, according to Gothard's teaching, one act of disobedience, even an unintended act of rebellion against authority, could result in God's punishment. Gothard taught that by rebelling we were subjecting ourselves to the realm and power of Satan.

My teenage self would see other young people suffering or struggling spiritually and assume their pain was a result of some rebellion against their parents. If something difficult happened to me, I'd think I'd stepped out from under the umbrella because I'd unknowingly disobeyed or disrespected my parents. My understanding was the result of Gothard's teaching that the main role of authority figures is protection—not control: "The essence of submission is not 'getting under the domination of authority but rather getting under the protection of authority.'"[2]

Of course, Gothard taught that God was life's ultimate authority. But to live under the umbrella and enjoy a flourishing life, you had to obey, respect, and honor the four human institutions to which God had delegated His authority: parents, government, church leaders, and employers.[3] Gothard said Christians who disobeyed even one of these authorities would no longer be under the umbrella of protection and would instead find themselves under the domain of Satanic attack.[4]

In some ways, it was easy to live under the umbrella. Doing so turned my Christian life into a simple checklist: *Did I break a law of the state of Arkansas today?* If the answer was no, I was still under the umbrella. *Did I listen to my spiritual authorities and commit to obeying what they said?* Yes. Still protected. Finally, and most dominant in my life, was the daily question: *Have I done everything my parents asked me to do? Have I obeyed them with a cheerful, happy heart?*

This simple, black-and-white view of authority relieved some of my insecurity and indecision. For example, when I couldn't decide whether I should play broomball or stay home and read my Bible, my dad took away a lot of my confusion when he told me I should go play broomball. As silly as it sounds, broomball became a matter of obedience to a God-given authority in my life. Since my dad wanted me to go, I was safe under the umbrella. In the same way, when I was struggling with body image and nearly stopped eating, my mom lovingly told me I had to eat. This made maintaining a healthy lifestyle a matter of obedience. There are many similar examples when my parents' authority was used for good in my life. I know their leadership often protected me from harm.

Yet, though I did not realize it at the time, Gothard's teaching was creating serious issues in how I understood God and reality.

## PROBLEMS WITH THE UMBRELLA OF AUTHORITY

As I look back on my teenage years, I wish I had spent more time studying what the Bible says about authority. It has so many good things to say about parents and pastors and all the authority figures God has placed in our lives. But if I had taken a more careful look at the Bible, I would have found that the umbrella of authority is not an idea presented within its pages. Gothard led me to believe that any little misunderstanding or misstep with my authorities would result in spiritual or even physical harm. Though I know authorities are there for my good and often my protection, their authority is not absolute. Only God's is. I often got that backward when I was younger. Gothard's theology so emphasized obedience and submission to authority that I began to believe all authorities—whether parents or Gothard himself as our spiritual leader—were never to be questioned or challenged in any way. They were simply to be obeyed. This had seriously negative effects.

## Self-Righteousness

Gothard's teachings led me to believe that God was mainly pleased with me due to my obedience. I didn't outwardly rebel against my parents or any other authorities that were part of the umbrella. In return, I expected God to pour His blessings on me.

One time, while my family and I were attending a conference led by Gothard, we saw a billboard that criticized him and his teaching. I remember thinking it was so sad that someone could be that blind to the truth. *They don't understand. They don't know what I know. They aren't as fortunate as I am.* I told myself the person responsible for that billboard had a heart of rebellion and was going to endure a lot of hardship in life. At other times, I'd hear about young people who grew up believing the same things I did but then rebelled by listening to worldly music or wearing immodest clothes, and I'd expect God to punish them in a way He never would punish me. They were no longer listening to authority, while I was fervent in my obedience. I was safe under the umbrella of protection. They had stepped out from under it and were opening themselves up to Satan's attacks.

Gothard emphasized obeying authorities so much that I began to think "obey" was the most important command in the Bible. My Christian life became a transaction with God rather than a relationship with Him: *If I obey the authorities in my life, then God will be pleased with me and bless me. If I disobey those authorities, God will not be happy with me and will not bless me.* I had figured out this formula for receiving God's blessings. I felt sorry for anyone who didn't know about Gothard's principles; because they didn't know anything about his teaching, they weren't going to experience the same joy and satisfaction that I would.

Throughout my teenage years, this self-righteous attitude was a big part of my identity. I was a fervent believer in Gothard's principles, and I thought I was pleasing God because I followed them zealously. I now see how that self-righteousness made me a lot like the Pharisees—the religious leaders of Israel during Jesus' life on earth. The Pharisees believed themselves to be righteous people who were committed to obedience. But they were all about outward performance. Jesus said, "They do all their deeds to be seen by others" (Matthew 23:5). They missed the whole point of knowing God. Like them, I was obsessed with outward performance and judged others who didn't follow the same rules I did.

## Fear

As I talked about earlier, I was a fearful kid. I was terrified of seemingly everything: weather, car crashes, sickness, and other people's perceptions of me. When I became a true Christian, those threats became much less threatening than God Himself. The thought of displeasing or dishonoring God was, at times, an all-consuming terror. Gothard's teachings gave me a practical, specific path to please God, but what his teachings didn't do—and this is so critical—was give me the right view of God's authority. Even as these principles were giving me a system that I thought would please God, the ever-present umbrella of authority was teaching me to be afraid of God.

Being afraid of God is different from fearing Him. The Bible says that fearing God is a good thing, something that brings joy and peace.

I know now that when the Bible talks about fearing God, it isn't talking about dread. It isn't telling Christians to think God is scary and terrifying. It isn't saying I should stay up at night with a knot in my stomach, afraid that God is going to punish me if I unknowingly break a rule. Instead, when the Bible talks about fearing God, it's talking about being in awe of Him.

Author Jerry Bridges described this well:

Perhaps a good working-definition of the fear of God is something like this: to truly fear God means to be in awe of God's being and character as well as in awe of what He has done for us in Christ. When you put these two ideas together, you have an absolutely sovereign Creator of the universe who punishes those who resist Him, and yet loves us and sends His Son to die in our place. Surely that's good reason to fear or reverence Him.[5]

That's such a helpful truth. It teaches me that the appropriate fear of God isn't because He could hurt me, or even kill me. The right fear of God is because He is all-powerful, in control of everything, and, at the same time, kind, compassionate, and loving. A being with that combination of qualities should be first feared for His character.

Gothard didn't teach me to be in awe of who God is and what He's done, especially through Jesus Christ. Instead, he taught me to focus primarily on God's punishment. I learned to fear what God could do to me. While the Bible affirms that authority has a place in our lives, Gothard turned obedience into a matter of terror. If I misstepped in any way, I was removed from all protection, and Satan would have full access. "As long as you are under God-given authority nothing can happen to you that God does not design for your ultimate good," Gothard said.[6] This implied that if I stepped out from the umbrella—knowingly or unknowingly—anything that happened would *not* be for my ultimate good.

That's why I was so passionate in my commitment to absolute obedience to my authorities. But that passion came from a wrong view of God, a terror of His authority and punishment, and therefore a wrong view of my earthly authorities. Gothard's teaching on this subject was tailor-made to produce that kind of fear.

## THE DANGER OF EXTREME AUTHORITY

Bill Gothard may have coined the "umbrella of authority" concept, but he was certainly not the first person to promote or exercise this kind of authority—the kind that assumes a leader gets to give orders. The kind where it's the leader's job to tell others what to do, and the people they are leading must obey with joyful hearts. This leadership structure is top-down. Those in charge should be served by those being led.

There are extreme examples of this kind of authority, like Jim Jones, who led the Peoples Temple. Jones convinced more than nine hundred people that it was God's will for them to move to Guyana in Central America, where they attempted to set up a utopia, an ideal society where they could live in harmony until Christ's return. Of course, that didn't work. We are all imperfect, so no society can be a utopia. When some members of the congregation tried to leave, Jones stopped them. Then he convinced his people to drink Kool-Aid laced with cyanide. Tragically, 918 people died in what became known as the Jonestown massacre.[7]

Thankfully, most people are not told that to obey their leaders, they must take their own lives. But leaders still display this top-down view of authority in other ways. Perhaps a boss abuses his authority by demanding more work for less pay. This leader is frustrated when employees don't do things exactly as he says, or he keeps asking for things that make his life easier but are not part of someone else's job description. Maybe a church leader insists that he should have the final say over where someone works, who to date and marry, what clothes to wear, and what music to enjoy. On top of that, he starts to imply that disobeying him is the same as disobeying God. Finally, and most personally, this shows up in a lot of families. Some parents don't just have opinions about their kids' lives; they have commands. Even when their kids are all grown up, these parents expect to be obeyed in all things.

What's a person to do in those situations? How do we respond to those authorities in our lives?

## TRUE BIBLICAL AUTHORITY

I've spent more than a decade trying to disentangle a true understanding of authority from the false version Gothard taught. I had to learn what the Bible really says about authority and leadership. I'll always be amazed when I read the thirteenth chapter of John's gospel. In this passage, Jesus did not demand that His followers serve Him. He did the opposite. He took a towel and a bowl of water and washed His disciples' feet. At that time, everyone wore sandals and walked on dirt roads. When the head of the house came home, his servant would bend down and clean his feet. Therefore, the task was associated with servanthood. And that's why Jesus did it. When He finished washing His disciples' feet, Jesus told them, "You call me Teacher and Lord, and you are right, for so I am. If I then, your Lord and Teacher, have washed your feet, you also ought to wash one another's feet. For I have given you an example, that you also should do just as I have done to you" (vv. 13–15).

Incredible. Here was the greatest man who ever lived. The Savior of the world. The King of kings and Lord of lords. No one has ever had more authority than Jesus. But what did Jesus do with all His authority? He washed His disciples' feet. He served His followers.

When James and John, two of Jesus' most loyal followers, asked Jesus if they could rule with Him in heaven, Jesus told them they had a wrong view of leadership. He said,

> You know that those who are considered rulers of the Gentiles lord it over them, and their great ones exercise authority over them. But it shall not be so among you. But whoever would be great among you must be your servant, and whoever would be first among you must be slave of all. For even the Son of Man came not to be served but to serve, and to give his life as a ransom for many. (Mark 10:42–45)

Bill Gothard, along with many other religious, business, and political leaders, taught the opposite of what Jesus said: that people in high positions *should* exercise authority over those they lead. I used to assume that was true. Now I understand that James and John should have asked Jesus how they could help others flourish, not what they needed to do to gain power. The same is true of leaders today. The leaders I want to follow, and gladly obey, are those who do not want "to be served but to serve."

Leaders serve not only those they lead but also God: the One who gave them their leadership. They are accountable to Him. This is so important! A leader without accountability is not a true leader. God does not give parents, presidents, pastors, or CEOs the freedom to lead however they want. They are accountable to God, and if they are abusive leaders, they will face consequences. We see a good example of this in Ezekiel 34, where God chastised the leaders of Israel for not serving their people.

What did God do about these dominating, abusive leaders? Ezekiel said God was going to rescue His people from them. He made it clear that God hates it when leaders abuse their authority.

When that happens, God promises to free His people from their harmful leaders.

God took away these leaders' positions and authority. He held them accountable. I've learned now that when I encounter a spiritual leader, I have to ask two questions: First, are they servant minded? Do they understand their role? Second, are they accountable to God? Do they go beyond the Word of God in their commands and expectations? Do they understand that there are limits to their leadership?

I didn't truly understand this nature of leadership when I was younger. Because I misunderstood what a leader is, I didn't examine any of Bill Gothard's teaching. I assumed he was a spiritual authority—a prophet-like figure—and thought God wanted me to follow him.

I don't know what would have happened to me if I stayed under the umbrella of authority and closely followed the rest of Gothard's principles throughout my life. I know it would have been exhausting to try to please God by obeying man-made rules. Perhaps at some point the effort would have been too much. It was for thousands of Gothard's followers who have left Christianity entirely because the rules were too much of a burden. I might have joined them.

Thankfully, when I was twenty-one years old, my life, and my view of Gothard's teachings, started to change.

# CHAPTER 5

## An Outside Voice

*On December 21, 2013,* I turned twenty years old. I wish I could remember what I did to celebrate. After all, it wasn't that long ago. But for some reason, details like this get lost in my memory bank. I do remember what I did the next year on my golden birthday. To celebrate twenty-one years on earth, and all the privileges that come with it, my mom and dad took me to Red Robin. I had never been before and haven't been back since. Afterward, we went to a few stores. This was nothing glamorous but clearly more memorable than whatever I did the year before.

What is seared in my memory from my twentieth birthday is that when my teenage years ended and a new decade began, there was little doubt in my mind that the next ten years would set the course for the rest of my life. My older brother had already married. I even had a niece and nephew. I assumed my other older brother, sisters, and I would soon follow in marriage.

As I waited for Mr. Right, travel occupied my time. Our reality show provided opportunities to see the world. When I wasn't traveling for the show, I was going on mission trips, both in the States and internationally. Once a year, several members of my family would visit a maximum-security prison in Florida. We'd bring Bibles and books to the inmates. We'd show them a curriculum called Journey to the Heart from Bill Gothard's ministry. These booklets talk about the conditions of the heart. We were trying to help the inmates identify their wrong heart attitudes—like complaining or bitterness—and replace them with positive heart attitudes—like joy and contentment.

After going through a Gothard booklet, we'd sit at tables and talk about how the female inmates could practically apply what they'd just learned. At the time, I thought this was a wonderful, useful ministry. I'd talk about having healthy attitudes and perspectives, maintaining joy during difficult trials, and taking responsibility for our actions. I'd also discuss God's design and how He had something special planned for everyone. I felt good about the difference I was making—helping these ladies understand how they could improve themselves and their circumstances.

So much has changed since then. Now when I remember those trips to Florida and think about the women with whom I spoke, I'm filled with regret. I wish I hadn't spent those brief hours talking about decisions, attitudes, and perspective. It was borderline silly for someone like me to talk to prisoners about decisions they could make that would improve their circumstances. Instead, I wish I'd taken those opportunities to tell the inmates how they could be truly free even while they were in prison. I wish I had talked about the radical love of Jesus Christ. Those women needed to hear about grace, forgiveness, and the hope of eternity.

Along with doing prison ministry in Florida, each year our family took at least one trip to the IBLP headquarters near Chicago and spent time with Gothard. Every trip to headquarters was a highlight. I considered Bill Gothard my hero, so any time I got to spend around this man of God was a thrill. I was certainly "starstruck" when my siblings and I would get to talk to him. He even came to our house once. We cleaned it for about a month in anticipation of his arrival. A few days before he showed up, the place probably smelled of bleach. Here's a journal entry from a few days before he came. I was twelve years old at the time.

> I am going to try to play Foosball with Mr. Gothard when he comes here with the fifty mayors from different countries. I can hardly wait for when Mr. Gothard comes here!!!!!!!!!

The nine exclamation points say it all. I was excited. And he really did bring fifty Romanian mayors with him. I think he was supposed to be some kind of spiritual mentor for those political leaders. And yes, I did get to play Foosball with him. Here's my journal entry the day after he left.

> It was a VERY, VERY GOOD time. It was AMAZING!!! Only six Romanian mayors were Christians!! It was really a neat privilege having Mr. Gothard here at our home. He also took time to play Foosball before he left! Jess and Mr. Gothard against Jill, Josiah, and me. Mr. Gothard's team won!!

I was so eager to please, I was actually thrilled to lose. At the time, it didn't really matter whether Gothard was playing a game, discussing leadership with mayors from Romania, or teaching the Bible: I was always eager to listen.

He always talked passionately about some new teaching he'd recently discovered. Sometimes the breakthrough had to do with a Christian discipline. He'd claim to have discovered the secret to prayer or the profound and previously overlooked physical, mental, and spiritual benefits of fasting. I remember him once talking about a new diet. He said that by connecting different ideas in Scripture for the first time, he had figured out what kind of food every Christian should eat if they wanted to live a long, healthy life and enjoy God's blessing. Whatever Gothard was promoting, it was convincing and inspiring.

About three months before I turned twenty, I had probably my most memorable visit to the IBLP headquarters. Here's what I wrote in my journal on September 18, 2013:

> So this afternoon, Jana and I were at the Staff Center, and Mr. Gothard asked us if we'd like to go out for dinner with him and some of the staff. We agreed and said we'd meet him back there at 7:00 p.m. Well, it started raining at 6:45 p.m., right before we were to head over there. Just then, my phone rang and he offered to come pick us up. Up he came in his beautiful blue car. They hopped out and opened the car doors for us. We even drove right past Boston Market! We went to a restaurant called Omega. We had a wonderful time of discussion! It was truly a blessing getting to spend quality time with a man of such great wisdom. That was one of the most incredible experiences by far! I am so thankful to God for Dr. Gothard's ministry. If it wasn't for his obedience to God, I would more than likely not be here! We serve a powerful God! Another topic discussed tonight was how can we reach the most amount of young people in the time we have left here. I pray that God will expand the impact of the godly influences of our day.

Yes, the Boston Market reference is a little odd. But that was Gothard's favorite restaurant. So it was a big deal when we drove past one, heading to a nicer restaurant. I certainly left Chicago that year with a fresh, new way of thinking about the Christian life. At the time, I didn't realize that I was also leaving Chicago with more commands to follow and rules to obey.

After those meetings in Chicago, we'd drive to Michigan for Journey to the Heart: a seven- or ten-day retreat mostly for young people ages thirteen to thirty. The program was also used in prison ministry. It focused on the heart conditions that people must have to experience God, understand who He is, and live out His expectations. Throughout the summer, and a few other times during the year, IBLP ran this program from the Northwoods Conference Center in Watersmeet, a small town in Michigan's Upper Peninsula that felt like it was hours from civilization. Sometimes I was there to learn. Other times, I went to serve in the kitchen. There was a massive lake at the center of the property that I'd often circle on long prayer walks. One week I memorized the book of James. I still remember most of the book to this day. I'm incredibly grateful for that. The program was intense, and at the end of it, I did think I was closer to God.

Most years, I'd also travel to El Salvador and Honduras, where we'd visit local churches and try to help them in any way we could. We'd run programs for children. We'd deliver Christmas gifts. We'd take groceries to families in need. I looked forward to these trips each year. The Christians in both countries were kind, joyful, and loving, even though they had so much less than most Americans.

When I wasn't involved in ministry, I was usually filming, either at home in Arkansas or on the road. My late teens and early twenties were a particularly busy season with the show. They were the last few years of *19 Kids and Counting*. The episodes became more invested in the lives of us kids as we became adults and started to court. We did a show with Habitat for Humanity in Alabama. We spent a month filming in Europe, the Middle East, and Asia. We did a wilderness survival camp. We spent a month in Tennessee, helping our friends build an addition to their home.

All the travel introduced me to many people who were different from me—including Christians from different backgrounds. The time on the road was a good introduction to adulthood and a season of life that I look back on with gratitude.

## GROWING UP DUGGAR

While our family was on the road, young girls would often introduce themselves and ask us for advice. Many of them were trying to figure out how to navigate relationships with parents, friends, and, of course, boys. My three older sisters—Jana, Jill, and Jessa—were getting the same questions, so we decided to write a book. We thought of it as a way to continue those conversations and start new ones. The result? *Growing Up Duggar.* This book was published in March 2014 and became a *New York Times* bestseller.

Our book was "all about relationships"[1]—with parents, siblings, friends, boys, and God—but much of its content was influenced by Gothard's principles. In that book, I explained how Gothard's seven basic principles applied to my life. The idea of the umbrella of authority made it into the book. So did some of Gothard's reasons for why girls should dress a certain way, avoid different kinds of music, and watch out for witchcraft in movies.

We also included a lot of content about how to have a successful life. I don't see the same road map for success today that I saw then. I mostly see a young girl who needed to learn a lot more about God, the Bible, and life before claiming to have answers. Here are a couple examples of ideas that I was so confident about when I wrote the book but now find to be unhelpful. They could even be harmful.

In a section on making wise choices, I was critical of one of the most wholesome TV shows of all time: *The Andy Griffith Show.* A couple pages later, I talked about the history of rock and roll, a topic I had not studied thoroughly.[2]

For a girl who was barely out of her teenage years, I had a lot of confidence. I was sure I knew about a lot of topics. The older I get, the more I realize how little I actually knew and how hesitant I should have been to urge readers to avoid certain shows or musical genres.

In the spring of 2014, my sisters and I went on a book tour to promote *Growing Up Duggar*. We signed books in places like Chattanooga, Tennessee; Harrisburg, Pennsylvania; Raleigh, North Carolina; Alexandria, Virginia; and Birmingham, Alabama. We enjoyed traveling the country together, and we met a lot of young girls at each stop. Most thanked me for the show or book. Many told me they'd started wearing long skirts because we wore them on the show. Others told me they planned to court instead of date when it was time to consider marriage. They were especially grateful for our clean, wholesome values.

At the time, nearly all these conversations encouraged me. They made me feel like I was making a difference. Because of the show— and my commitment to Gothard's principles—lives were being changed. Young girls were becoming more modest, pure, and virtuous.

Less than a year later, I realized something important was missing from most of those conversations. I was neglecting to tell those girls an essential, life-changing truth. Today, I'd have a much different message for those girls and a much different response when they told me about the external changes they had made because of the show and *Growing Up Duggar*.

I wish I could tell them that I should not have emphasized man-made rules so much in my first book. I would try to help them understand that the Christian life is about Christ. It's not about clothes, dating guidelines, or music. I'd probably point them to Romans 14:17 to remind them that "the kingdom of God is not a matter of eating and drinking but of righteousness and peace and joy in the Holy Spirit."

Because soon after the book tour, my life was turned upside down and transformed. The change started when my best friend met the love of her life.

## FRONT-ROW SEAT TO NEW PERSPECTIVES

Though I get along with all my sisters, Jessa has a special place in my heart. She is my closest sibling in age, only thirteen months older than me. She is fifth and I am sixth of nineteen Duggar kids. Growing up, Jessa and I were together all the time. Though all the Duggar girls shared the same room, I often felt like I was roommates with only Jessa. Our beds were next to each other for my entire childhood. We did everything together. After finishing our schoolwork, we played card games, drew, or went shopping. When our massive family went on trips, Jessa and I always stuck together.

I think we get along well because we complement each other. We aren't carbon copies. Jessa has a stronger personality than I do. I often hesitate to speak my mind and share my opinion. Jessa is the opposite. If she doesn't understand something or doesn't agree with what she's hearing, she's not afraid to ask questions or disagree. When I was a teenager, I couldn't imagine speaking my mind with as much boldness as Jessa. She also has an outgoing spunk. She doesn't get nervous when she meets new people. I love Jessa for who she is. I've learned so much from her as we've navigated life together.

A few months before Jessa and I went on the book tour for *Growing Up Duggar*, seventeen-year-old Ben Seewald walked into our church in Arkansas. He had seen the show a few times and, he admitted later, thought Jessa was cute. The church service might not have been his focus that particular Sunday. Jessa was twenty years old. At the time, that seemed like a big age gap, but Ben wasn't intimidated by an older girl. Jessa felt the same spark of interest as Ben. Their relationship started in the middle of 2013, not long after they met. They were together for eleven months before Ben asked Jessa to marry him. They tied the knot on November 1, 2014.

As Ben and Jessa's relationship became more and more serious throughout 2014, they started taking trips to the Seewalds' home a few hours away. Under the courtship rules, they couldn't make these drives alone and needed a chaperone. I was the obvious choice.

Thankfully, Jessa and Ben were always kind to me. They didn't seem to mind having me along, and I enjoyed being the third wheel, having a front-row seat to the first year of their relationship. And I was literally in the front seat of Ben's small truck. From the moment we started the drive until we arrived at Ben's home, the conversations didn't stop. Occasionally, I would jump in, but most of the time I was happy to just listen. Jessa and Ben talked about everything, and I loved how honest they were with each other. They talked a lot about their faith during those car rides. Theology—the study of God—was probably the most popular topic. What is God like? How does He redeem people? What does it look like to obey Him?

## A New Perspective on Scripture Verses

Anytime Ben would explain something during his conversations with Jessa, he would quote an entire passage of the Bible to make his point. He didn't pick one verse to support an idea. He let Scripture speak for itself.

I don't know if I'd ever heard someone treat the Bible that way. Most of the Bible teaching I heard from Gothard was topical in nature. Though Gothard wasn't a pastor, and he lived more than five hundred miles away, his teaching featured prominently in the home churches I attended each Sunday morning. In these settings, my family and a few others would gather to sing and learn. Sometimes a father from one of the families would share a devotional. Other times we'd watch a video of a Gothard seminar or another Bible teacher.

Bill Gothard would pick a subject and tell us what he thought the Bible said about that topic. He would begin a seminar with a problem, then he'd find a solution to the problem in a verse or two. He'd spend the rest of the seminar—sometimes sixty to eighty minutes—giving his opinion on what that verse meant and how it applied to our lives.

Of course, Gothard made it seem like his opinion was synonymous with the Bible's teaching. Once he convinced you of Scripture's command to obey him, he'd say you needed to take a vow to follow what he'd just said. Through this process, he would use Scripture only to make whatever point he wanted to make.

Because I'd spent so much time listening to Gothard, I thought individual verses in the Bible were best used as evidence during arguments. I had memorized lots of them as my defense for what I believed. Of course, single verses can be helpful, but they don't explain everything the Bible is saying. The Bible is a book. You don't take one sentence out of a book and make it say what you want—or assume that, based on the one sentence, you know what the entire book is about.

As I chaperoned Jessa's new relationship, I realized that Ben didn't do that. He would talk about entire passages of Scripture, not just a verse or two. He would carefully reason from the text. He talked about what the Bible meant—not always what it meant for him or how it could be applied. His perspective on the Bible was different from mine. I didn't realize at the time how much I was learning from Ben. I wouldn't understand how much I was benefiting from those car rides until I met Jeremy and we started having similar conversations. Jeremy also had this amazing Bible knowledge, and I was eager to talk to him about Scripture. I think my eagerness was there because of what I heard during those drives with Ben and Jessa.

Starting with those car rides and going through my relationship with Jeremy, I would learn that I needed to stop asking myself what the verses I was reading meant to me and instead try to figure out what God was saying about Himself. When I did that over the coming years, I would begin to see that the Bible is more interested in telling me who God is than giving me guidance for every small decision I make. God is the main character of the Bible; I am not. I had never thought about the Bible that way. I honestly hadn't considered that it was God's story. This was the beginning of a massive perspective change in my life.

## A New Perspective on God's Sovereignty and Glory

I'll never forget Ben and Jessa's conversation about the sovereignty of God—the idea that God oversees everything. He rules over the earth, both nature and humans. Over the next few days, I looked for places where the Bible talks about God ruling over creation. They were everywhere. Here are a few of my favorites:

- "How great are his signs, how mighty his wonders! His kingdom is an everlasting kingdom, and his dominion endures from generation to generation" (Daniel 4:3).
- "I am God, and there is no other; I am God, and there is none like me, declaring the end from the beginning and from

ancient times things not yet done, saying, 'My counsel shall stand, and I will accomplish all my purpose'. . . . I have spoken, and I will bring it to pass; I have purposed, and I will do it" (Isaiah 46:9–11).

- "Are not two sparrows sold for a penny? And not one of them will fall to the ground apart from your Father. But even the hairs of your head are all numbered. Fear not, therefore; you are of more value than many sparrows" (Matthew 10:29–31).

- "For by him all things were created, in heaven and on earth, visible and invisible, whether thrones or dominions or rulers or authorities—all things were created through him and for him. And he is before all things, and in him all things hold together" (Colossians 1:16–17).

- "The lot is cast into the lap, but its every decision is from the LORD" (Proverbs 16:33).

I had read those verses and the passages around them before, probably multiple times throughout my life. But until I started to focus on God when I read my Bible, I didn't have a category for God's sovereignty. I hadn't truly understood what these verses were saying: I am not in charge of my life. I don't get the credit for anything good that happens to me. Suffering and hardship come from God. My sin and foolish decisions may contribute to them, but ultimately, suffering comes my way because God sent it.

God graciously opened my eyes to see His sovereignty all over the Bible. It seemed that every passage I read was saying the same thing: God is in charge. In my journey away from the teaching of my youth, this was the first step: a realization that the Bible places God at the center. God is the ruler of the universe.

As I read, I also started to pick up on new elements of God's glory. He didn't create the world because He was lonely. He created it to increase the fame of His name.

God's glory was the focus of entire chapters in the Bible. This was another big change in my thinking. I'd always thought my job was to be a light to the nations. I wanted others to look to me and want the successful life I had. Now I saw that my job was to point others to God. His glory was more important than anything.

## ANOTHER WAY TO DO THINGS

As Ben and Jessa's sidekick, I would visit the Seewalds for two or three days at a time, mostly over weekends. From the first time I met them, Ben's parents made me feel like I was already part of their family. His mother, Guinn, is one of the kindest, sweetest women I have ever met. She loved hosting Jessa and me, and she always made us feel right at home.

The Seewalds made an impression on me, specifically because they didn't dress the same way I did. The women wore pants. They listened to music I didn't. Ben and his siblings were homeschooled like we were, but they were part of homeschool co-ops. The girls worked outside the home. So much of their lifestyle and decisions didn't line up with how I thought Christians ought to live.

A lot about the Seewalds' church was different as well. Their pastor simply walked the congregation through the Bible. He explained what a passage meant when it was originally written thousands of years ago. He didn't preach sermons about topics. He let Scripture speak for itself.

I left each service wanting to hear more. There was an exciting sense of freedom and satisfaction that came from simply knowing more about the Bible. I started to see changes in how I thought about God. I started to see how He was working in the world and how big and powerful He was compared to how small and weak I was. I wasn't yet ready to question everything I believed—not even close. But I was ready to consider the possibility that someone who didn't know anything about IBLP or Bill Gothard could be truly following Jesus and living a meaningful, joyful, God-honoring life.

My conversations with the Seewalds were the first step on my journey of disentangling wrong beliefs. The next step began when I met a man who bravely upheld the Bible to show me why my beliefs were not biblical. Not long after Ben and Jessa got married, this man became a part of my journey—and a permanent part of my life.

# CHAPTER 6

# Life-Changing Conversations

*I don't remember* exactly how many guys asked my dad if they could court me. I know it was at least twenty. It could have been as many as twenty-six. I'll never forget the week that five young men approached my dad, asking to start a relationship with me. I don't share that number to brag. It doesn't say much about my personality, character, or looks because most of these guys didn't know me. Some had seen me at a conference my family attended. I hadn't shared more than a passing hello with any of them. I'm guessing a few confused me with one of my sisters. Several had seen the show and decided they wanted to court a Duggar girl. A similar number of guys were interested in each of my sisters.

Thankfully, my dad always asked me and my sisters what we thought. If we didn't want to court a guy, our dad would go back and let him know there was no interest. I'm not going to lie; it was kind of nice to tell my dad, "Thanks, but no thanks," and not have to tell the suitors themselves.

Jeremy was the last guy to ask my father if he could court me. He was unlike the previous guys in nearly every way. He didn't pursue me because I was a Duggar. He wasn't a fan of the show, and he knew next to nothing about the tight-knit, conservative Christian circles in which I'd grown up. Jeremy and I met at IBLP in Big Sandy, Texas, but he was not there to attend or to meet me. He came to spend time with Ben and Jessa.

When Jeremy showed up at that conference in 2015, he was a former professional athlete who had attended not one but two universities. After college, Jeremy played professional soccer in Finland, New York, and Texas. He had traveled around the world and lived in many places, giving him a background that was vastly different from mine. None of my family was that serious about sports. And none of us considered going to a university—especially not liberal, secular schools like Hartwick College or Syracuse University. On top of all that, Jeremy was from Pennsylvania, not far from Philadelphia, which felt like a completely different world from Arkansas!

Along with Jeremy's different background and interests, his theology and convictions were different from mine. While I was a follower of Bill Gothard's principles, Jeremy was raised by a Reformed Baptist pastor. Some of his views on the Bible, God's character, and the Christian life didn't line up with what I had been taught. Those differences initially made my parents hesitant to approve our relationship. Thankfully, Jeremy has a lot of perseverance. He was determined to win over my parents, which he did after five months of almost weekly conversations with my dad.

During those five months, Jeremy watched Bill Gothard's seminars so he could better understand what I believed. He didn't know much about Gothard, but Jeremy was a student of the Bible, and he was confident he'd benefit from all that instruction. And if watching the seminars helped him win over my dad, all the better. Jeremy watched more than sixty hours of IBLP content. He started with the Advanced Seminar, which goes deeper into the seven basic principles. Then he went back and listened to the Basic Seminar, which introduces the principles. He also listened to more than twenty hours of the Financial Freedom Seminar. He took pages and pages of notes as he listened.

By the time my parents gave me and Jeremy permission to court, he had a lot to say about Gothard's teaching. I was eager to talk with

Jeremy about his beliefs relating to God, His Word, and salvation. Those sweet conversations with Ben, Jessa, and the Seewalds had helped me understand that a faithful, God-honoring Christian life didn't have to look exactly like mine. The Seewalds clearly loved the Lord, and I felt the same way about Jeremy. Though his theology was different from mine, his character was obvious. He loved the Lord and was eager to obey Him. I trusted Jeremy, and for the first time, I was ready to hear a different perspective on the Bible.

## A FRESH LOOK AT FAMILIAR TEACHING

During our courtship, Jeremy was a pastor in Laredo, Texas, and I was living at home in Arkansas. We talked on the phone all the time. Though having a long-distance relationship was hard, I'm grateful for all those hours of conversation. When you have nothing else to do but talk, you learn a lot about the other person, going in-depth on topics you might otherwise gloss over. That was certainly the case for Jeremy and me.

I was a bit intimidated by Jeremy when we started dating. The first time we really spent time together was on a mission trip in Honduras and El Salvador. Ben and Jessa had pulled some strings to get Jeremy on that trip so he and I could spend some time together and we could see if there was any spark between us. Though Jeremy didn't know a lot of people on the trip other than me, he not only took an interest in all the team members, he also provided a lot of biblical encouragement and insight to everyone on the team. His natural leadership impressed me.

The mission team would gather in the evenings for Bible study, and the leader would facilitate a discussion, encouraging the group to ask one another questions. Someone would ask for wisdom with a difficult family situation. Another would ask for help with a passage of the Bible they didn't understand. The topics were wide-ranging. Anyone from the group could offer answers. Whenever Jeremy spoke, I was always impressed by how biblical, wise, and loving his answers were.

By the time Jeremy and I started having those phone conversations six months later, my respect for him had only grown since that trip to Central America.

In one of our first conversations, Jeremy told me he had been listening to Gothard's seminars and asked me what I thought of his teaching. I don't remember what I said. But I do remember being eager to hear Jeremy's opinion on Gothard. So I turned the question back on him. I'll never forget his response. Jeremy said that Gothard had some good things to say—some helpful insight into life—but Gothard approached the Bible from a philosophical point of view. He was not a Bible teacher. *Not a Bible teacher?* I thought. That was absurd. Bill Gothard was *the premier* Bible teacher in the world. Why would Jeremy say he didn't teach the Bible?

A year or two earlier, when I was helping write *Growing Up Duggar* and then going on a tour to promote the book, I probably would have ended the conversation as soon as Jeremy said Gothard wasn't a Bible teacher. At that time, I wouldn't have been ready to hear someone say something like that. But so much about me had changed during the past twelve months. The Word of God truly had become sweeter to me and also far more powerful and compelling. I was beginning to see the glory and greatness of God for the first time. My understanding of God's character was slowly evolving.

I was now open to different views on Christianity from the one I'd always known. So when Jeremy said he didn't think Gothard was a Bible teacher, I was willing to hear more.

During the next several months, Jeremy and I listened to

Gothard's seminars together on video calls. We'd often pause the video and talk about what we'd just heard. The first thing I started to see was that Gothard did not teach the Bible correctly. I began to understand how his teaching was feeding my fears and guilt, not showing me the grace of Jesus.

## Superstition

One of the first times Jeremy and I paused a Gothard lecture to discuss what we were hearing was after Gothard told a story about a woman who lived many years ago. Tragically, she became a widow and childless when her husband and three sons went off to sea and never returned. A pastor stopped to comfort her, but while he was there, he didn't provide comfort. Instead, he accused her of being the reason her family had died. He pointed to a painting hanging on her wall of a sailing boat and said, "The problem is the picture over the mantel." He said, "If you didn't want your boys to go out to sea, you should've gotten rid of the picture for the sake of your children."[1]

Gothard used this story to argue that you have to be careful about everything, including the art you put up in your home. You may, without realizing it, cause your family to do something destructive because they were inspired by a painting you chose to hang in your home.

When I heard this story while listening with Jeremy, I was horrified. I couldn't believe that in front of thousands of people, Gothard said this pastor was right to blame the death of those three sons on their mother's choice of art. The pastor was not kind and compassionate. He didn't care for this woman and try to comfort her in the midst of unimaginable grief. Instead, he placed an unimaginable burden on this heartbroken woman! She had not only lost her children but was now being told their deaths were her fault.

Something she'd thought was innocent—a painting she hung on the wall—was actually murderous. And then Gothard used this pastor's callous response as an example of the right thing to say to the woman. He commended him for his response and used his words as a warning for the audience.

As Jeremy and I talked about this story, I realized I had been captive to superstition most of my life. It was a major source of my fear. For a long time, I believed that at any moment, God could be displeased with me for some hidden reason. For instance, I was worried that I might hear music that would make God angry. Once I was in the car with some friends who started listening to music that, at the time, I was sure didn't honor God. I was genuinely scared that I was going to get in trouble with God for even hearing it.

I also fretted about my clothes. I remember one time feeling a lot of guilt because I had worn a skirt that I considered immodest. When I sat down, the skirt did not fully cover my knee. Here's what I wrote in my journal that night:

> The Lord has been convicting me about modesty. A few times I had on a borderline knee-length skirt that would come above the knee when sitting. God brought conviction to my heart in this area. These "small things" are often some of our greatest battles. Especially challenging when others around me, Christians included, aren't doing what I've been convicted of. Not to have a heart of pride thinking I'm better in any way but just walking with a meek, humble attitude toward God and those around me.

A few days after this journal entry, I went shopping for longer skirts. I scoured thrift stores looking for skirts that would drop well below my knee. I wanted to be as modest as I could possibly be.

That was a terrible way to live, and it's not what God intended.

He doesn't punish us for random nonsinful decisions we make. He is far kinder. He tells us exactly what sinful behavior looks like. Here's a straightforward command from God's Word: "Do not lie to one another, seeing that you have put off the old self with its practices" (Colossians 3:9).

If God doesn't tell us in the Bible that something is sinful, then He gives us freedom to decide whether or not we want to do it. For example, since the Bible doesn't say anything about boat paintings, I'm free to put up such a painting in my house. God isn't going to punish me for that decision.

## Salvation by Works

Another place in the seminars where Jeremy and I stopped the audio to discuss was after Gothard described a conversation he had with a young girl who had grown up in church but stopped believing in God. Here's what Gothard said to that girl when she told him she wanted to return to God:

> "It would be unfair for me to ask you to become a Christian knowing that Jesus Christ would come into this kind of a mess in your life. Unless I had a way for you to get from wherever you are on this scale [of perversion] back down to freedom by very clear steps back down to genuine love, genuine freedom."
>
> She looked at me, and she said, "Do you have a way?"
>
> I said, "I sure do!" That's what the gospel is all about. That's what the apostle Paul was talking about in Romans chapter 7 and verse 8. Paul said, "Before I saw the holy law of God, I thought I was living a normal life. But then when the law came it slew me, it revealed in me all manner of concupiscence. It promoted in me that" [speaker's paraphrase] because he saw where he should be and where he couldn't get, and so it just made him all the

more awkward about the concupiscence—sin. "The law revealed all manner of consequences in my life." And yet the apostle Paul says to us in Romans 6 [vv. 13–14, speaker's paraphrase], "If you obey from the heart the form of doctrine that I'm gonna give you, then sin shall not have dominion over you. And that we would be able to be perfectly free [if we obey]."[2]

After describing this girl's sin and mistakes in detail, Gothard convinced her to ask, "Do you have a way?" In other words, she was asking, "How can I escape my destructive life, be saved from my sin, and become a Christian?" That is the most important question anybody can ask. Because it's the defining issue of Christianity, few mistakes are more damaging than telling others the wrong answer, misleading them, or lying about how God saves. Sadly, that's what Gothard did. He said that before this woman could follow Jesus, she had to first clean up her life because Jesus couldn't "come into this kind of a mess in your life." In other words, this woman needed to start behaving better. She needed to obey and do good works for a while before God could save her.

Jeremy and I talked about how this is *not* the gospel of Jesus Christ. It's the opposite. The Bible is clear that good works can't save anyone. The book of Isaiah says that our good works—righteous living—are nothing more than filthy rags (64:6). Romans 3:10–11 says, "None is righteous, no, not one; no one understands; no one seeks for God." If we had to clean up our act and obey for a while before God would save us, then we would never be able to obey enough to earn God's salvation.

Instead of earning God's grace by cleaning up our act, the gospel says we simply must believe. Believe what? That Christ saves all who call on His name. Acts 16:31 says, "Believe in the Lord Jesus, and you will be saved." No one earns salvation by cleaning up their life, as Gothard told that young girl. We come to Christ with all our mess, and Jesus does the cleaning. He transforms sinners who hate God into saints who love Him and are motivated by that love to obey Him.

Since the gospel of grace is the most important message in the world, parents' most critical job is to explain the gospel to their children. I'm thankful my parents did that. If I or my siblings asked them how to be saved, they would say that our good behavior couldn't save us. Only Jesus and His finished work on the cross could do that. Even before I became a Christian at the age of fourteen, I remember hearing Mom and Dad talk about the grace of God. One of the great blessings of my childhood is that my parents pointed me to Jesus' grace when they talked about becoming a Christian. I'm sure that if I had asked Gothard how to get to heaven, he would have talked about the grace of God. He probably would have said that salvation wasn't something I could earn. But he was often adding works to grace, as he did with that woman. I'm thankful that even though my parents were influenced by Gothard, they didn't tell me what he told that woman. They didn't tell me I needed to clean up my life before becoming a Christian.

The stories of the painting and the woman who Gothard told to clean up her life are two examples of moments in Gothard's seminars that Jeremy and I discussed, but there were dozens more. We spent hours combing through this teaching that had consumed my youth.

## Communion

As I previously shared, I used to be convinced that I might die if I took Communion while not knowing about a sin. Most Sundays, I wouldn't take Communion because I was afraid. I would think, *What if I have a sin I can't remember? What if I remember that sin later? Or God knows about it and I never figure it out? If that's the case, I'll be judged for taking Communion.* The littlest conflicts would lead me to skip the Lord's Supper. For example, if I needed to apologize to my sister for my attitude, I wouldn't take Communion. This was pure superstition.

As Jeremy and I listened to Gothard's recorded sermons, I understood for the first time why I struggled with this overwhelming fear of Communion. During a discussion about the Lord's Supper, Gothard explained that if we had a secret sin we had yet to express, it would bring physical destruction. It was very important that we thoroughly examine ourselves.[3]

Of course, Scripture warns believers not to take Communion if they aren't ready for it. First Corinthians 11:27–30 says,

> Whoever, therefore, eats the bread or drinks the cup of the Lord in an unworthy manner will be guilty concerning the body and blood of the Lord. Let a person examine himself, then, and so eat of the bread and drink of the cup. For anyone who eats and drinks without discerning the body eats and drinks judgment on himself. That is why many of you are weak and ill, and some have died.

That passage used to terrify me because I didn't understand that it is not telling believers to stop remembering their Savior through this joyful act; it's telling Christians to stop using Communion as an excuse to party, get drunk, and divide the church. The apostle Paul warned believers to stop abusing Communion, but he would never tell a sinner to stay away from something designed to remind them of their salvation.

I used to think of Communion as an act of accountability. I thought God gave it to Christians like me to make sure we weren't sinning too much. But in 1 Corinthians 11:26, just one verse before the warning about those who eat and drink in an unworthy way, the Bible says, "For as often as you eat this bread and drink the cup, you proclaim the Lord's death until he comes." Taking Communion is a reminder to believers and all the world that Christ died, rose again, and is coming back to earth.

Gothard's wrong view of Communion is another example of how his teaching twisted the Bible and made me believe God is harsh toward His children—a common takeaway from his teaching. I started to think that God was always out to get me, whether that was in Communion or in other areas of life, including activities as ordinary as eating.

After Gothard urged his audience to examine themselves, lest they die, he said this:

> The tragedy is we live in a fallen world, and many times we do things in our life that we're not even aware that we're getting judged because we're not searching out the Scriptures.[4]

This was a terrifying idea for me when I was younger. The idea that God was judging me for mistakes I didn't even know I was making kept me on edge a lot, wondering if I was accidentally disappointing God. Right after Gothard said this, he applied it to food. He said that a lot of people eat food that God doesn't approve of, and they don't know it. The example he used is bread: I'm supposed to eat just the right amount of fiber in my bread. If I don't, God is going to judge me for it. Ideas like that filled me with uncertainty.

I now see Gothard's teaching on Communion and food as examples of his superstitious Christianity. Believers who followed Gothard's teaching not only needed to wonder if the paintings they hung would cause them harm but also needed to be paranoid that there was some secret spiritual harm lurking in the food they ate.

I used to worry that all kinds of food could be spiritually harmful to me. I was hesitant to eat foods like pork, shrimp, clams, oysters, crabs, and lobster. Anything Leviticus deemed unclean. In one of his seminars, Gothard pointed to Luke 8:33, where Jesus cast demons out of a man and they went into a herd of pigs, to make a point that pigs have an unclean spirit and are not supposed to be consumed by men.[5] Consequently, when I was a kid, I thought I would be disobeying God if I ate pork.

I didn't realize at the time how much of a burden it was to worry about the bread I ate and the pork I avoided. Gothard was making food more important than it's supposed to be. He was making eating a burden because I had to figure out what food was spiritually pleasing to God and what food was not.

Now I know that God has given us all food to enjoy. As 1 Timothy 6:17 says, God "richly provides us with everything to enjoy." Food is there to sustain us. It's also a gift.

## The Danger of Making Yourself "Essential"

What is the overarching theme of these examples that Jeremy and I heard? It felt like Gothard was cultivating dependence on himself. He seemed to be manipulating his audience by saying, essentially, that God's Word is not clear. That there are hidden dangers in the world, dangers most people don't know about, that can cause spiritual harm. These dangers could come in paintings, Communion, food, and even confessions. As Gothard set up all this superstitious Christianity, he presented himself as the only one who could identify those hidden dangers and steer his helpless audience in the right direction. He talked again and again about having the "keys to success" in the Christian life. He claimed his principles would unlock the full potential of Christianity.[6]

Now I see that this kind of teaching made Gothard essential

to his listeners. If there are secret principles that lead to God's favor, and if Gothard alone understands those principles, then he is an essential teacher. I believed that growing up. I was sure other Christians didn't have success in life because they didn't know Gothard's basic life principles.

During my experience of disentangling truth from error, I have learned to be skeptical of any leader or teacher who claims to be essential. If a teacher says the Christian life can only be lived successfully with some secret bit of knowledge they have discovered, then that teacher should be avoided at all costs.

Thankfully, God, in His kindness, does not keep us in the dark. His Word is clear. The key to the Christian life is not listening to hours of lectures from Bill Gothard. It's knowing Jesus Christ. And Christ is not hidden. There's no secret way to access Him. He is clearly presented in the Bible, not just the four Gospels— Matthew, Mark, Luke, and John—but in the entire Bible. Jesus is prophesied about and foretold throughout the Old Testament. And He is explained and exalted in all twenty-seven books of the New Testament. Jesus is the key to the Christian life. And the way to unlock His riches is to know Him through His Word.

As my relationship with Jeremy grew and I started to think more clearly about Christianity, I realized that I did not know some of the Bible's most important truths. I was about to begin an extraordinary education.

# CHAPTER 7

# A Season of Learning

*Once Jeremy and* I had my parents' permission to court, we were excited to be together and talk seriously about marriage. Though we only courted for three months and were engaged for three months, our first half year together was full of many highlights.

I'll never forget my first visit to Laredo in June 2016, a few weeks after we began courting. I went with my parents, and Jeremy's mom and dad came from Pennsylvania for the weekend. It was my first time meeting them, and they were as kind and thoughtful as Jeremy described. My parents also enjoyed the time with Chuck and Diana. The conversations were easy and enjoyable. I loved seeing Jeremy's church for the first time and meeting so many members. We got to eat a lot of great food. Laredo is on the US-Mexico border, so there's all kinds of great Tex-Mex there. We explored downtown, visited Jeremy's apartment, and experienced the extraordinary heat, which slaps you in the face the moment you step out of the airport. By the end of the trip, I was even more convinced that Jeremy was the man I was going to marry.

Not long before Jeremy asked me to marry him, he showed up in the most surprising way. I was at a Mexican restaurant in Fayetteville with Jessa, Ben, and their son, Spurgeon. I ordered tacos, and instead of a waiter bringing them to me, Jeremy delivered the meal (then, of course, he joined us). I'll never forget the shock. I did a double take, and, for a moment, nothing came out of my mouth. What followed was a sweet visit and at least a few days where we could talk in person rather than over the phone.

As much as my relationship with Jeremy was changing my life throughout the summer of 2016, I don't think it was that year's most significant change. Instead, as Jeremy and I approached marriage and talked about the Bible for hours and hours, I learned a lot about Scripture. Even though I'd loved and appreciated it for years, I hadn't dug as deeply into its truth as Jeremy and I did during this time. And the best way to explain what happened during those calls, how my understanding of what the Bible is changed, is to talk about the end of a Gothard seminar and the vows he asked his audience to make.

## THE GOTHARD VOW

The last few minutes of a Bill Gothard seminar were almost always serious, sobering moments. No laughs. No jokes. No music. Gothard's trademark smile would vanish. His eyes would narrow. He'd return once again to something he referenced throughout each seminar: vows.

If Gothard referenced the dangers of alcohol during his seminar, he wouldn't wrap things up until he asked the audience to vow never to drink alcohol or even be in the presence of someone who did. If he talked about the dangers of rock and roll, he'd tell his audience they needed to vow before God never to listen to such music again. There was even a script for this personal commitment.

And if Gothard's seminar stressed the importance of modesty, he'd urge everyone in the crowd, especially females, to commit never to wear anything immodest. Sometimes this came in the form of a specific vow never to wear pants, shorts, or miniskirts. And never to wear sleeveless or low-cut shirts.

By far the most common vow Gothard asked his audience to

make involved Bible reading and prayer. He didn't ask for a big sacrifice: five minutes of Bible reading and five minutes of prayer every day. He made it sound so easy. He implied this was the least Christians should do to show God they were committed to Him. Gothard would ask for a show of hands—a public commitment to the vow. Hands would go up all over the room. Then more hands. Eventually, so many raised hands blanketed the room that seemingly everyone in attendance—thousands of people—were making the same vow.

Whether someone raised a hand because of peer pressure or because of a genuine desire to read Scripture and pray more often, they were now committed to something Gothard said was deadly serious. He would point to texts like Deuteronomy 23:21: "If you make a vow to the LORD your God, you shall not delay fulfilling it, for the LORD your God will surely require it of you, and you will be guilty of sin." What were the consequences of that sin? Gothard had a few ideas. He said God would cause suffering, sickness, or even death if someone didn't keep a vow to the Lord.

I'll never forget the conference where I personally made this vow about Bible reading and prayer. The pressure to do so was overwhelming. Everyone around me was making the same commitment. Plus, there are 1,440 minutes in a day. The vow was only requiring me to dedicate ten of them to the Lord. How hard could it be?

In the coming months and years, that simple vow would haunt me. If I didn't read my Bible or pray in the morning, I'd feel so much guilt. Sometimes at night, I'd realize I hadn't fulfilled my vow. Lots of nights, I'd see one of my siblings reading the Bible in our room and freak out, scrambling to read a chapter or two before I went to bed. The difficult thing about that vow wasn't the length of time required; it was the relentless nature of the guilt. The vow weighed on me. Even if I did read my Bible and pray first thing in the morning, I'd only have to wait a few more hours for that same pressure and guilt to creep back in.

Of course, reading the Bible is a good idea. Psalm 119:11 says, "I have stored up your word in my heart, that I might not sin against you." There are too many benefits of reading God's Word to count. So the problem wasn't with the object of my vow: Scripture and prayer. The vow itself was the problem. It was creating unnecessary guilt. God tells me to dwell on His Word, to "hide it in my heart," and to know it and know the One who wrote it. But nowhere does He command me to read the Bible every day. Laying that burden on myself was unnecessary.

A vow like that—especially one that calls for only five minutes each of those two crucial spiritual disciplines—is built on a serious misunderstanding of what the Bible is.

## THE BIBLE

If someone asked you to describe the Bible, what would you say about it? Maybe you'd describe its contents: a collection of sixty-six books divided into two sections, the Old and New Testaments. Those books were written by different authors over many centuries. Some wrote in Greek. Others in Hebrew. A few wrote in Aramaic. There are works of history, prophecy, and poetry. Many of those sixty-six books, especially in the New Testament, are letters.

All of that is the kind of definition you'll find in *Encyclopaedia Britannica* or on Wikipedia. And that description is accurate, but it leaves out the most important thing about the Bible: it was written by God. Christians believe the Bible is inspired, or God-breathed. God inspired every word written by the men who authored each of the sixty-six books. Second Timothy 3:16 says, "All Scripture is breathed out by God and profitable for teaching, for reproof, for correction, and for training in righteousness." Because the Bible is inspired by God, it has no errors.

Growing up, I was taught that the Bible is inerrant and infallible (though those words weren't often used). *Inerrant* means it doesn't have any mistakes. Every word of it is true. *Infallible* means there isn't even a possibility that it could have a mistake.

Here are a few descriptions of the Bible that I believed:

- The Bible is a road map for life.
- The Bible is heavenly words for earthly living.
- The Bible is a divine rule book.
- The Bible is like the owner's manual for a car.
- The Bible is basic instructions before leaving earth.

When I read the Bible, I believed I was reading the perfect words of God. But here's what I want to address: Why did God give us the Bible? That's the question I was confused about. I suspect that question confuses a lot of people, including Christians.

I assumed God gave us the Bible to show us how to live. He had a bunch of commands for His creatures. In the Bible, He laid out those commands so people like me could know with perfect clarity what decisions were good—would please God and bring success—and what actions were evil—would dishonor God and bring failure.

## WHAT THE BIBLE IS NOT

I now see that my understanding of the Bible changed in two phases. It started to change during those car rides with Ben and Jessa. Those conversations began to cultivate a perspective that would become more established as my relationship with Jeremy grew. During that time, it became clear to me that rules are not the only reason the Bible exists. Those who read the Bible only to figure out how to live—only to learn what rules to obey, what actions to take each day, and what bad attitudes and decisions to avoid—are missing the main reason the Bible was written.

I can remember lots of mornings reading the Bible and thinking, *How does what I'm reading apply to my day?* I'd think through my schedule. *I will be filming today, so how can the Bible help me say the right words or have the right attitude? I'm going on a trip with my siblings, so what does the text I'm reading have to say about my relationship with them? I'm about to pick my outfit for the day. The Bible can help me make sure I pick a modest outfit.* Of course, the Bible does help me in all those areas. But if that was the only reason I read the Bible, then I was missing a lot.

## Seeing the Bible As a Divine Rule Book

When Bill Gothard talked about the Bible, he talked about it as a divine rule book. His seminars hardly say anything about God's character, the way of salvation, the nature of the church, or dozens of other issues the Bible emphasizes. Instead, he taught me that the Bible is about me. It's there for my purposes. God gave it to me to show me how to be successful and happy. Believing that, I inserted myself into the story whenever I read the Bible. I assumed that every story in it had direct and specific application to my life.

The famous and dramatic story of David and Goliath, as described in 1 Samuel 17, is a great example. When every soldier in the army of Israel refused to fight the giant Goliath, David, a young shepherd, volunteered to fight him with only a sling and five smooth stones. The battle was over almost before it started when David slung the first stone at Goliath and hit him in the forehead, knocking the giant to the ground. David then killed Goliath with the giant's own sword. When I read that story, I asked only one question: *How does this apply to my life?* I assumed the answer was in the details. I'd read that David didn't wear armor when he fought Goliath and think, *What does that mean for me?* I'd read about the five smooth stones and think long and hard about the significance of that number. *Why weren't there six stones? What does that mean, and why is that number significant for me?* I'd see that the enemy was a giant and think, *Are there any giants in my life that I need to defeat?*

Here's another example, this one from a note I wrote next to Proverbs 23:1–3 in my Bible. That text says:

> When you sit down to eat with a ruler,
> observe carefully what is before you,
> and put a knife to your throat
> if you are given to appetite.
> Do not desire his delicacies,
> for they are deceptive food.

Every time I read that passage now, I shake my head at my application from years ago. I wrote "fasting" next to those verses. I decided God was using those verses to tell me I needed to fast.

But that's not what this passage is about. Instead, it's warning people not to be enticed by a rich ruler who will use his wealth to get them to do what he wants. That has nothing to do with fasting, but I thought I had to find a personal application for that text, so I came up with fasting. At the time, I genuinely thought this idea came from God. If I read the verse and thought of fasting, that must be God's intended meaning of that text for me. In other words, I believed that God had a specific, individualized interpretation for me.

## Looking for Rhemas

Bill Gothard called these personal interpretations of Scripture *rhemas*—communication from God to one person and no one else. The IBLP website defines a rhema as "a verse or portion of Scripture that the Holy Spirit brings to our attention with application to a current situation or need for direction."[1] Gothard claimed that rhemas had guided the IBLP ministry since it began. God had given him a new standard for the Christian life, and he had to start the seminars to make sure the world knew what he had discovered.[2]

When I'd visit the IBLP headquarters in Illinois, I'd frequently hear Bill Gothard talk to staff and guests about a rhema he'd received from the Lord. He would say God had used some portion of the Bible to tell him that a particular food was unhealthy or that a medicine would work wonders. (He regularly talked about food, medicine, and topics related to science.) He would say God had revealed a new principle through a rhema, and now he understood a key to the Christian life that was going to transform how we all lived.

I assumed the same thing was supposed to happen to me when I read the Bible. I was hoping to discover a hidden meaning that would be revealed not through words but through thoughts I would have as I was reading those words.

Gothard's rhemas weren't limited to the Bible. He also saw God communicating His will through personal experiences. Gothard would tell a lot of stories. He'd tell his audience about conversations he'd had, people he'd met, and accounts he'd read. Typically, these stories were about conflicts in relationships, alcohol abuse, financial ruin, or sexual immorality. In them he'd find analogies from everyday life. He'd say that because the person he was describing had conflict, alcoholism, debt, or a child out of wedlock, God was saying not to live like they lived in other areas.

Here is a story I was told more than once when I was growing up based on Gothard and other teachings. It shaped me in a profound way. It was about a young girl who stopped following Gothard's modesty standards. Soon, she started wearing pants and shorts. Gradually, her skirts got shorter, and her pants became tighter. As she dressed with less and less modesty, she became more and more interested in relationships with boys. At first, they were other Christians. But before long, she was dating non-Christians. Eventually, she became involved in a serious relationship with a guy who wasn't interested in God. He got her pregnant out of wedlock and left her to care for the child on her own. This kind of story was used like a weapon to warn girls against the dangers of dressing immodestly. They had lost their purity, marriage, money, and health after wearing pants—and that proved clothes could cause all kinds of heartache if not chosen carefully.

## Proof-Texting

When I was younger, I didn't realize that when Gothard told stories, he was finding truth in analogies, not in the Word of God. Only after he'd tell a story like this and describe the principle the story proved would he finally go to the Bible and find evidence for what he'd just argued.

This is called *proof-texting*. It's coming up with an idea you want to promote and using a smattering of verses to support your claim. People do this all the time, but when Gothard did this, I thought he was teaching the Bible because he would reference lots of verses. What he was actually doing was teaching his own ideas and then pointing to verses taken out of context as proof that he was right.

When I was talking with Ben and Jessa a year before Jeremy came into my life, we didn't discuss Bill Gothard and how much he had influenced my view of the Bible. When I eventually had those conversations about Gothard with Jeremy, I began to realize just how unhelpful—even dangerous—all of his proof-texting was. Ben and Jessa had helped point me to the truth, and Jeremy helped me understand when I was hearing something that sounded like truth but was actually off the mark. On a sidenote, I can see now how God has used people close to me to point me to His Word and His character. Those relationships are a kindness from God that I know He gives to His people. He certainly was kind to me in this way during this pivotal time in my life when so much was changing.

## Correlating

Of course, Gothard talked a lot about parenting during his seminars, so as Jeremy and I listened, we stopped and discussed having children. At one point, he asked me, "Jinger, how many children do you want to have?" Up until that point in my life, if someone had asked me that question, I would have said "as many as the Lord allows." But I was talking to the man I wanted to spend the rest of my life with, so I couldn't give him a vague, cliché answer.

I had to be honest. And I truthfully didn't know how many children I wanted to have. In fact, I was trying to figure out what the Bible actually said about how many children I was supposed to have. So that's what I told Jeremy. I appreciated his response. He didn't give me his opinion. He said he was thankful for my answer and we could figure that out later. So that's what we did. Then we turned the Gothard seminar back on and heard him say this shocking thing to the adopted men and women in the crowd:

> If you've been adopted, that means that God has an extra special purpose on your life. I can demonstrate that because look

at the many great men and women who were not reared by their birth parents. Here was Moses taken from his parents; here was Samuel turned over by his parents; here was Daniel taken away from his parents; here was Esther, she didn't have any parents; here was Timothy, lost his father. God says to you, "If you've lost your father or parents, I will be a father to the fatherless." God in special ways becomes your protection. But also, he brings you discipline because he's got this extra special purpose for your life.[3]

The Bible doesn't actually say Timothy lost his father (it simply implies that his dad didn't follow Jesus), but that isn't the biggest problem with Gothard's argument that God has a special plan for the adopted. The Bible never connects the significance of the figures Gothard mentioned with the fact they were not raised by their birth parents. Just because some of the Bible's characters were adopted does not mean God has a unique plan that applies only to adopted people. God's plan for adopted people is the same as His plan for everyone: to have faith in Jesus Christ and follow Him. To claim an "extra special purpose for your life" if you were adopted—or extra discipline from God for that same reason—is to deviate from Scripture.

This story is an example of a frequent mistake Gothard made: he built arguments around correlation. In other words, he would find connections in the Bible and tell his audience those connections proved some rule. This is dangerous because, similar to proof-texting, it allows the teacher to find whatever meaning he wants in the Bible. All he has to do is make a few loose connections from Scripture, and he can use those connections to say anything he wants.

## MY DISTORTED VIEW OF BIBLE STUDY

When I was younger, I'd open the pages of the Bible every day for at least five minutes, and two tragedies would happen. First, I'd heap burdens of behavior on myself. Looking only for direction for my life, I would come up with new guidelines or rules that I needed to follow. If I couldn't follow them as perfectly as I thought I was supposed to, I'd declare myself a failure. I would resolve to try harder. The next day, I'd repeat the process again. This was exhausting. It was the opposite of what Jesus said in Matthew 11:28–30: "Come to Me, all who are weary and heavy-laden, and I will give you rest. Take My yoke upon you and learn from Me, for I am gentle and humble in heart, and YOU WILL FIND REST FOR YOUR SOULS. For My yoke is easy and My burden is light" (NASB1995).

When I thought about my spiritual life, I didn't think about rest. Instead, I thought about all the things I needed to do and all the ways I had failed. The Christian life was a treadmill, and I was constantly picking up the pace, pushing myself harder and harder. But like a treadmill, there was no destination, no arrival point that signaled the end of all that pushing. There was just . . . effort. I'd fall off the treadmill from time to time, but I'd eventually get back on it. Such a self-focused, effort-driven spiritual life wasn't sustainable. I'm certain that if I didn't have the Holy Spirit—if I was not a child of God who was being protected by my heavenly Father—then I would have gotten off the treadmill and never gotten back on. I would have done what so many others have done when the hardships of life and the exhaustion of man-made religion become too much: abandon Christianity altogether.

The second tragedy fueled the first. Because I was placing myself at the center of the biblical story, I did not understand the actual story of the Bible. I could not answer basic questions about

Scripture like, "What are the Bible's key themes? Why did God create the world, including men and women like me? And what story is the Bible telling?"

Bill Gothard and others like him were too busy instructing me how I was supposed to live. He didn't take the time to explain the most important realities of the Bible.

## TRUE FREEDOM

It's easy to think that big events in life, like a graduation, relationship change, or near-death experience, will shape you and set the direction for your life. But big events were not the cause of my transformation. The Bible itself was. I finally understood why God's Word existed. I could trace its main story, and I knew that its main character was God, not me.

During those years, massive events were shaping my life and future. *Growing Up Duggar* was published. My best friend, Jessa, got married. I met the man I'd love forever. And my family faced the greatest crisis of our lives. But what changed me the most were the quiet moments when I read the Bible the right way. Reading the Bible became an exciting act of discovery that wasn't about me but about God and His glorious plan for the universe. As I focused on Him, so much guilt fell away, and Jesus became more precious to me than ever before.

I finally understood, for the first time, what true freedom is. John 8:36 describes it perfectly: "If the Son makes you free, you will be free indeed" (NASB1995). I also knew there were going to be fundamental changes to how I lived. And not all those changes would be accepted by the community that had raised me.

# CHAPTER 8

# Freedom from Fear

*I began to* seriously consider writing this book in the middle of 2021. As I did, I wrestled with fear, wondering what would happen if I publicly criticized Gothard-like teachings. Would I hurt relationships with friends and loved ones? Would people I cared about stop talking to me? Would they say I had abandoned the faith of my childhood—that I was at risk of walking away from the Lord? I worried I wouldn't be invited into homes where I had once been treated like family.

I thought about the IBLP conferences I'd attended as a kid. They'd been the highlight of the year. Some of my fondest memories are on the IBLP campus in Big Sandy, Texas. My siblings and I would ride bikes from one end of the property to the other. It was the only time of year we'd see all our friends from other IBLP families. We'd stay awake well past our usual bedtime, playing games and talking. It was fun getting to be with so many friends my age who shared the same beliefs. By criticizing Gothard and his principles, I worried I wouldn't be allowed back into a setting like that.

No one wants to be criticized by the community that raised them. But conservative, tight-knit religious groups can be particularly harsh to those who decide to leave. This fear of being labeled an outsider is an incredibly effective tool. Leaders use fear to keep people in line and ensure their loyalty. Give someone a sense of belonging, a group of people to share life with, a commitment to a cause, and an enemy to defeat, and you have a powerful recipe for loyalty.

# WHAT IS GOD LIKE?

So how did I overcome my fear to write this book? There are two answers to that question. The first one starts where the previous chapter ended: with the Bible's main character.

Once I understood that the Bible is about God and not me, the next question I asked myself was, "What is God like?" I knew He was holy. I knew He was just. I knew He was in charge of all creation. But I began to understand God as my heavenly Father.

Sure, I had always understood that God is a Father. That idea is all over the Bible. I knew verses like John 14:6, where Jesus said, "I am the way, and the truth, and the life. No one comes to the Father except through me." I didn't let that truth change me. Yes, I wanted to please God and, at times, I would feel close to God. But I just didn't think very often about His heart and fatherly care *for me*. Instead, I spent a lot of my energy focused on His rules for me. I did not understand verses like Psalm 68:5 or Psalm 103:13 or Romans 8:15.

God loves His children. He cares for us. He wants what is best for us. In fact, He promises to work all things together for our good (Romans 8:28).

In *Knowing God*—one of the books I heard about from Jessa's husband, Ben—author J. I. Packer shares a great description of how I now think about my relationship with God.

> You sum up the whole of New Testament religion if you describe it as the knowledge of God as one's holy Father. If you want to judge how well a person understands Christianity, find out how much he makes of the thought of being God's child, and having God as his Father. If this is not the thought that prompts and controls his worship and prayers and his whole outlook on life,

it means that he does not understand Christianity very well at all. For everything that Christ taught, everything that makes the New Testament new, and better than the Old, everything that is distinctively Christian as opposed to merely Jewish, is summed up in the knowledge of the Fatherhood of God. "Father" is the Christian name for God.[1]

Packer concludes, "Our understanding of Christianity cannot be better than our grasp of adoption."[2]

Growing up, I thought a lot about God as my judge. I thought about Him as the lawgiver and ruler of this world. But I didn't think much about Him as my loving heavenly Father. He adopted me into His family. That's an incredible privilege that I didn't understand.

As I started to think more about God as my Father, I was drawn to this passage in the Gospel of Matthew:

> Ask, and it will be given to you; seek, and you will find; knock, and it will be opened to you. For everyone who asks receives, and the one who seeks finds, and to the one who knocks it will be opened. Or which one of you, if his son asks him for bread, will give him a stone? Or if he asks for a fish, will give him a serpent? If you then, who are evil, know how to give good gifts to your children, how much more will your Father who is in heaven give good things to those who ask him! (7:7–11)

God, the Creator of the universe, wants to give His children good gifts. He does that every day through His creation. He gives us the world to enjoy, including the food we eat, the beauty we experience, the people we interact with, and the love we share. But by far the greatest gift He has ever given us is His Son, Jesus Christ. To truly understand who God is, I had to understand Jesus.

# WHO IS JESUS?

As I started to look for Jesus when I read the Bible, I noticed things about Him that I hadn't before. Jesus is full of compassion. He restored sight to the blind. He made the lame walk. He fed the hungry. He even brought people back from the dead. He was not afraid to spend time with the worst sinners. He is eager to forgive anyone who repents. He is full of mercy and compassion. He is gentle and lowly. Most profoundly, He is the Savior of the world.

If I had to sum up my search to understand God, who He is and what He's like, I'd say I found that in the cross of Calvary. A few years ago, I heard a description of the cross that I think describes it so well: The cross is where God's perfect justice and mercy meet. When Jesus was crucified, He paid for the sins of all who would ever believe in Him. That means you and I can have our sins forgiven if we simply have faith in what Jesus did for us.

At the cross, Jesus took the punishment we deserved. Here's one way I've heard it phrased: God the Father was punishing God the Son for the sins of God's children. See what I mean about perfect justice and mercy? There's no greater news in the world. Jesus' death on the cross freed me from the consequences of sin. I don't ever have to worry that God will punish me for my mistakes and disobedience—past, present, or future. Because I don't have to face the wrath of God, I can also enjoy freedom from all other fears. Why worry what others think about me if God loves me as my Father? Why worry that I won't have what I need if God controls everything and has promised to provide for me as His child? Why worry about what will happen in the future if God has promised that I will one day live with Him forever in heaven?

With this understanding, the things I used to assume would displease God—taking Communion when I wasn't supposed to or playing broomball instead of praying—no longer made me afraid of Him. If He was willing to give up His Son for me, He wasn't going to then punish me for a sin I didn't know about or playing a game with my family.

## HOW DOES MY NEW UNDERSTANDING HELP ME WITH MY FEARS?

I still struggle with fear from time to time. There may always be nights where I lose sleep because I think someone is disappointed in me or upset by a decision I've made. And if someone I love has a serious health issue, I'll no doubt feel that familiar knot in my stomach. I may struggle with fear for the rest of my life. But I now see my fear differently. I know that God doesn't promise to remove it if I have enough faith. He promises to help me when I do feel that familiar fear. In other words, God doesn't promise to remove all sin and struggles—but He does promise to be my refuge during every trial.

Forty-two times, the book of Psalms says God is a refuge for His people. For example:

- Psalm 46:1 says, "God is our refuge and strength, a very present help in trouble."
- Psalm 61:3–4 says God is a refuge against the threat of enemies: "For You have been a refuge for me, a tower of strength against the enemy. Let me dwell in Your tent forever; let me take refuge in the shelter of Your wings" (NASB).
- Psalm 71:1 says, "In You, O LORD, I have taken refuge; let me never be ashamed" (NASB1995). That verse is particularly powerful for someone like me who struggles with shame.

Instead of dwelling on my shame or trying to ignore it, I can take it to God.

- Psalm 142:4–5 describes a person who went to God and found refuge from loneliness: "Look to the right and see; for there is no one who regards me; there is no escape for me; no one cares for my soul. I cried out to You, O LORD; I said, 'You are my refuge, my portion in the land of the living'" (NASB1995).

The final Psalm I'll share is, I think, the most practical. Psalm 91:1–2 says, "He who dwells in the shelter of the Most High will abide in the shadow of the Almighty. I will say to the LORD, 'My refuge and my fortress, my God, in whom I trust.'" When I am in trouble—when I feel like fear and anxiety are overwhelming me—this verse tells me what to do. I speak to God. I pray. I praise Him for being "my refuge and my fortress." I tell Him that I am going to trust Him. And I believe that He will not allow the fear to consume me.

## HOW HAVE I LOOSENED FEAR'S GRIP?

This clear understanding of the gospel is the primary reason I was able to loosen fear's control and commit to writing this book. The second reason is concern for the people I know and love who also grew up in the Gothard movement.

Most followers of Gothard's teaching are people who sincerely want to follow God and please Him. And when you are trained to fear the outside world, you do whatever it takes to avoid it. You embrace everything Gothard says, no matter how difficult or frustrating it can be, because the obedience is assuring. It gives you a sense of righteousness and safety. The pitfalls of the world cannot touch you if you truly believe and always obey.

Yet many of my friends and acquaintances are now in difficult circumstances connected to their upbringing in the IBLP world. Their commitment to following Gothard's rules has kept them from having healthy relationships with others and understanding who God is and what He's truly like.

Imagine this scenario: A man and woman get married. They immediately start having children because Gothard opposes any kind of birth control. Financially, they are not in a position to own a home because they're not allowed to go into debt. That means no mortgage. So they live in what they can afford: a tiny, two-bedroom house that they rent. At first, that's okay because they have only one child. But then more children come. Next thing they know, they're six years into marriage with five children under five years old. To provide food and clothing for his family, the husband works longer hours, taking on more responsibility or even more jobs. This takes the dad out of the home for ten or twelve hours a day. Since they're not allowed to send their kids to school, the mom is in her home, with morning sickness from pregnancy for half the year, trying to manage and homeschool five kids. She feels overwhelmed, unable to handle the responsibility of raising so many children practically alone.

Then the husband comes home, and the house feels like chaos. But the wife has to have it all together to keep her husband faithful and satisfied. That's what Bill Gothard taught her. The house must be clean, she must be happy with no expectations, and the children must be well-behaved. The problem is, she's struggling to maintain her mental health and physical appearance, which is terrifying because it means her husband may start desiring other women. The guilt begins to build. On top of that, she is told she must be joyfully available to meet her husband's physical needs. More sex likely means more children, but they are told, over and over, to *just trust God*.

Sadly, this is not a hypothetical scenario. It's a difficult situation many people have experienced after buying into Gothard's principles. Gothard, by the way, never married and never had children. How did he become the leading authority for so many issues he himself never understood?

Unfortunately, Gothard's principles were also problematic for those who, like Gothard, never married. Women were told, by Gothard and others, that marriage and child-rearing were God's primary purposes for them. As the years passed and they remained single, many of these women believed life was passing them by. They felt worthless, like they couldn't fulfill their God-given purpose until a man took interest. While they waited for marriage, they could not start a career or even go to school because women were supposed to care for the home. They needed to remain at home under their parents' authority, no matter their age, submitting to their fathers' leadership and control.

So many I know and love have decided Christianity is not for them because all they ever knew was Gothard's version of it. They assume God is oppressive and overbearing, just like Gothard's theology. When they see so-called Christians treating others poorly, and leaders like Gothard accepting it, they think God is like that too. My heart goes out to them. I can understand why they don't want anything to do with Christianity. I'm writing this book because I want my friends in this situation to know that God truly is compassionate and loving. He cares for them. He sees their pain. And the life He wants for them does not look at all like the life Gothard prescribed.

## WHAT IS THE SOURCE OF TRUE FREEDOM?

Thankfully, the Lord has carried me through. He's given me a new understanding of Him and His Word. And He's given me many wonderful gifts I don't deserve, starting with my family. When Jeremy and I stood before our family and friends on our wedding day, November 5, 2016, we promised to love and cherish each other as long as we both live. I felt so much relief on that beautiful afternoon. Our wedding felt like the finish line, the end of a season of courtship that had more than a few challenges. But in reality, Jeremy and I were at the starting line, and we had no idea what God had in store for us.

There was no way of knowing all the joys and trials we'd face together in the coming years. I didn't know Jeremy nearly as well as I thought I did on our wedding day. Through trials like a miscarriage and a move across the country, I've seen a depth of compassion and godliness that has drawn me closer to Jeremy than I thought was possible before we said *I do*.

Jeremy is a servant leader who puts my needs and the needs of our daughters above his own. I thank God each day for my marriage. But on a deeper level, God has sustained my faith through trials, temptations, and questions. I've rejected so much of the religion of my youth, but I have not rejected Jesus. And I have only the Lord to thank for that.

I identify with the pain that many have experienced, especially the fear. And I think it's this fear that has driven so many to deconstruct their faith to the point where nothing is left. But although He has been misrepresented and His teachings applied the wrong way, Jesus is true, His love is real, and His forgiveness, kindness, mercy, and grace are the greatest blessings in the universe.

In John 8:36, Jesus said, "If the Son sets you free, you will be free indeed." That is the central message of this book. Jesus is the source of true freedom. Rejecting Christianity because it's associated with a teacher like Gothard may give the appearance of freedom, but it will not lead to true freedom. Likewise, obedience to man-made rules does not set anyone free. As Gothard would say, "Freedom is not the right to do what I want but the power to do what I ought."[3] Obedience like that gives a sense of freedom because it puts you in charge. But it doesn't take away the demand for constant obedience. Someone under a man-made religious system can never break free from the demands of that system. On top of that, man-made religions cannot take care of our main problem: sin.

Contrary to what I grew up believing, the ultimate threat to you and me is not the world. Instead, the ultimate threat to me is . . . me. I need freedom not from the influence of the world, not even from a religious system, but from myself. I am born enslaved by my own sin. Jesus said that in Matthew 15:14–20. This passage has been so helpful for me. Jesus was talking to His disciples—His twelve closest friends. They asked Him why He compared the Pharisees to blind guides leading blind people after the Pharisees accused the disciples of breaking their rules.

Jesus taught His disciples—and all of us—a crucial lesson about what is and is not the source of sin. In Matthew 15:11, he said, "It is not what goes into the mouth that defiles a person, but what comes out of the mouth; this defiles a person." Something external, like food or the influence of the world, does not make a person sinful. Having unclean hands does not make us spiritually dirty, as the Pharisees claimed. We are already messed up and infected by sin. The world can't make us more sinful than we already are.

The freedom we need is not from the world; it's from ourselves. Only Jesus can provide that. His death and resurrection free people from the consequences of their sin. One day, His death and resurrection will free people even from the presence of sin. My prayer is that people will stop focusing on their own efforts and look toward the true freedom, rest, and refuge that only Jesus Christ provides.

# WHERE IS THE LOVE?

The last time I attended an IBLP conference was April 2018. My parents were speaking at the conference on the topic of pursuing a dynamic marriage. Jeremy and I wanted to see them and the rest of my family. It's not always easy to coordinate time with them all at once, but the conference in Big Sandy provided that opportunity.

The conference theme was "Herein Is Love." That's a reference to 1 John 4:10, in the King James Version, which says, "Herein is love, not that we loved God, but that he loved us, and sent his Son to be the propitiation for our sins."

I don't remember all the sessions, but I know there were talks about family devotions, being a godly father, and the relationship between science and the Bible. My understanding of God and His Word had completely changed since I first met Jeremy at this conference back in 2015, so I was very aware of just how man-centered much of the teaching was. It was focused on life improvement. The topics were geared toward personal success, thriving relationships, and family dynamics. This was ironic, since God's character, particularly His love, is the entire point of 1 John 4:10. I don't remember hearing anyone define *propitiation* or explain how love finds its greatest fulfillment in the cross.

I was struck by just how much I had grown in my faith. It seemed like ages ago that this conference had played a massive role in my life. I used to think it was the greatest thing in the world that three to four thousand people would show up every year to Big Sandy, Texas.

I no longer felt that excitement. I realized the teaching was not focused on Scripture or the gospel, and I saw sadness in so many families I knew and loved. Many children who had grown up with me in IBLP were not at that 2018 conference. They had rejected

Gothard's teaching. And worse, they had also rejected Christ. They no longer called themselves Christians because what they were taught throughout their childhood proved ineffective. Staying in that bubble and far from the world's influence had not kept them away from their own flesh. They were still sinners. No amount of protection and rules could change that.

But Jesus offers freedom—true freedom. And when you understand His love, you will never be the same. I know I wasn't.

# CHAPTER 9

# Finding True Love

*When Jeremy and* I married, he was the pastor of a small church in Laredo, Texas. It was the first time I'd lived away from home. In fact, at the time, I was the only Duggar kid not living in northwest Arkansas. (Today there are two. Jeremy and I live in Los Angeles, and my brother Justin and his wife live in Texas.)

I felt ready to move out of state. I didn't foresee any issues being away from my family. My thoughts were centered on marrying Jeremy and starting a life with him. I assumed everything would be fine when we got to Laredo. I was wrong.

Not long after we settled into our new life, I found myself feeling anxious in social settings, including church. While I was genuinely excited to go to church on Sundays, I worried about the relational side of things. I had attended church nearly every Sunday since I was born, and I didn't remember ever feeling this way.

Like most kids who grow up in church, I'd experienced moments of indifference, weeks where there were other places I would rather be. But for the most part, I'd always loved attending church. I had visited all kinds of churches throughout my travels, and I had never felt anxious because I was with my family. They were my security blanket. In Laredo, my family was hundreds of miles away. I had to learn how to build genuine relationships on my own. I quickly realized I had no idea how to do that, which led me to feel a stomach-churning, palms-sweating, mind-racing kind of anxiety.

I should have felt the opposite. I had a newfound love for the Bible. I understood the story it was telling. I was engaging it like I hadn't before. I was also excited to worship God through song. On top of all that, I got to hear my brand-new husband preach every week. I know I am biased, but Jeremy is a phenomenal preacher. He explains the Bible accurately and with passion. I was grateful for the opportunity to listen to him do what he loves. His sermon was the most peaceful part of the service for me. The calm in the storm. The anxiety came before and after the service, when it was time to strike up conversations with other members of the church.

When someone from the congregation would approach me and ask the simplest question, like "How are you doing?" I'd stumble through a trite response. "I'm fine. How are you?" Most never knew that while I was giving them guarded, cliché answers, I was experiencing full-scale internal panic. My mind would hurl the same accusation at me again and again: *Don't say the wrong thing! Don't say the wrong thing! Don't say the wrong thing!* I didn't want to embarrass myself. If I was in a group, especially when I was with Jeremy, I didn't feel this social anxiety. It only paralyzed me during one-on-one conversations.

One of my lowest moments happened a few months after moving to Laredo. Determined to meet new people, make friends, and be a good pastor's wife, I scheduled brunch with a young mom in our church. She is one of the sweetest, kindest people I know. There was nothing threatening about her. Still, that morning I told Jeremy I couldn't do it. I cried right up until I left for the restaurant. I was terrified I'd say the wrong thing or wouldn't know what to talk about. I was worried that she wouldn't like me or would think I was weird and awkward.

Somehow, I managed to drag myself to the restaurant. I didn't bring an appetite with me. I ate my food but didn't enjoy it. I was nervous the whole time. From the moment we sat down together until we said our goodbyes, I felt like I could burst into tears.

Not long after that, my social anxiety caught up with me. I

was at the house of another lady from church, and she was asking questions to get to know me. I don't remember what she said that triggered my reaction—she was being sweet, thoughtful, and kind—but I suddenly started to cry. The pressure of figuring out what to say, combined with the fear of saying the wrong thing, became overwhelming. I couldn't keep back the tears. They started to pour out of me. My host was gracious and understanding. I don't remember what she said when she realized I was crying, but I remember her being gentle and patient. She prayed for me and gave me the space to talk or not say anything. I'm grateful for her understanding, and I wish I would have opened up a bit more to her.

Moments like that almost didn't feel real. They were more like out-of-body experiences. They weren't who I thought I was. Growing up, I was one of the most social Duggar kids, always with my parents or at least one of my siblings. I was an extrovert—the girl who wanted to live in a big city, surrounded by people. I was the kid who didn't mind talking to strangers. I'd walk up to people at stores and start telling them about Jesus. Starting in my teenage years, I'd traveled all around the world and met thousands of people. I'd spoken at conferences in front of large audiences. No anxiety in those settings. But put me in a cute brunch restaurant with a sweet friend from church, and I'd freeze.

## EXAMINING MY SOCIAL ANXIETY

Before moving to Texas, I can remember just a handful of times I'd gone one-on-one to coffee or a meal with a person who wasn't part of my family. I did not have many close friends who weren't also siblings. My sister Jessa was my best friend. Beyond her, I was, and still am, very close with all my sisters.

I was rarely in isolated social settings. At least one sibling or parent was always with me. When we traveled, filmed for the show, spoke in front of audiences, or interacted with people on mission trips, we did it together. My family was my security blanket. I was comfortable around them.

That dependence on family transferred to Jeremy as soon as we married. If he was with me, I was comfortable. He is incredibly confident in social settings, so I would follow his lead. But if Jeremy wasn't with me and I had to hold a conversation, I didn't know what to say. Part of that is because I simply had no practice.

Another reason those conversations were difficult was because I had always believed there is a right answer and a wrong answer to everything. Saying the right thing was part of being a light to the nations. I thought that by projecting confidence, knowing what to say, and always smiling, I would make my faith look more appealing to the world. I could do that in front of large crowds. It was as if there was a script to follow. The same was true on TV—I knew how I was supposed to talk and act when the cameras were rolling. When traveling for the show, a book signing, or mission trip, I would interact with a lot of people, but they were passing acquaintances. I would repeat the same clichés over and over during these introductions. And I was always with my sisters, so if I didn't know what to say, I could turn to one of them.

Getting to know someone by myself forced me out of that performative mindset. It put me in an unpredictable situation. Because I didn't know the other person, I didn't know what they expected me to say. I had no idea how to make them happy. I didn't know who I was, either, so I'd try to adapt to the other person's personality—or I'd freeze.

If life consists of moving from one script to the next, then life itself becomes a performance. That's essentially what Gothard taught me life should be. This lack of authenticity makes developing close relationships incredibly difficult. If I'm worried about saying the wrong thing, of stepping out of my role in the drama of life, then I can't get to know someone, and they can't get to know me.

Growing up, I thought I had to perform for the world, putting on a joyful, self-assured countenance at all times. For women particularly this expectation seemed to often extend to the home. In many of the families who attended Gothard's seminars, it was my impression that women would follow a specific script with their husbands. They would think it was their job to be agreeable and encouraging. Many of the women I interacted with seemed to make a point to avoid any topic that might lead to conflict. Why did Gothard teach women to always be agreeable? Because if they complained or argued with their husbands or failed to support them, those husbands would look to other women for support and submission.

Here is a summary of a story from one of Gothard's seminars where he described this horrifying perspective. It explains so much of my actions during my first year of marriage. A woman came up to him and asked him why her husband left him. Gothard had no idea. He implied that the woman was very attractive. As they talked, Gothard figured out that this woman never encouraged her husband. She was sad and critical of him. She didn't have a grateful spirit. If she had a grateful spirit, Gothard told the audience, she would still be married.

Gothard filled this story with drama and intrigue. He told the wife that he was sure her husband was going to leave her for a woman at work because that's where he was being complimented and experiencing female gratitude. From Gothard's perspective, a man is owed that kind of regular gratitude. If a wife doesn't regularly compliment him and talk about how wonderful he is, he can't be expected to stick around.[1]

Gothard made me believe that all men are like the one he described in this story. For that reason, I thought that when I married I was going to have to constantly encourage my husband or he was going to leave me. When I was younger I assumed that if my husband had an affair, it would be my fault. Yes, he would have messed up, but I would be to blame because I hadn't been the wife he needed to be happy and encouraged. Because that was what I assumed about marriage, I was scared I wouldn't measure up. I wouldn't be the kind of encouraging, happy wife my husband needed.

That first year of marriage to Jeremy, I may not have said I still had this perspective on marriage, but I acted like I was the one responsible for my husband's happiness and fidelity to me. For my entire life, I'd been taught that when I married, I needed to perform for my husband. Those instincts weren't going to disappear overnight, even though I had intellectually disentangled the truth that I should support, love, and encourage him from the error of thinking it was my responsibility to keep him faithful.

That first year in Laredo, I never expressed an opinion. It didn't matter how trivial the topic. When Jeremy asked me what I wanted for dinner, I would say, "Whatever you want is fine with me!" He'd get the same answer when he asked me what I wanted to do on a Saturday or how I wanted to spend a holiday. Even when he would ask me questions that he didn't really care about, like what color curtains to put in our house, I would say, "Whatever you want is fine with me!"

Sometimes I acknowledged Jeremy before I even knew what he was talking about. More than once while Jeremy and I were on a walk or sightseeing during a trip, he'd see something he liked and say, "Hey, Jing, look at that." Before turning my head and looking at what had caught his attention, I would exclaim, "Wow!" in the most upbeat, positive voice I could muster. I did that because I didn't think my opinion mattered. What mattered was gauging Jeremy's excitement and matching it, even in small things.

But Jeremy wanted to hear my opinion. He gently encouraged me to speak my mind and let him know if I didn't agree with something—and to not apologize for that. He didn't want me to perform or be fake. He wanted me to be myself. More than once he said, "Jing, you're not a Stepford wife."

The first time he said that, I asked, "What's a Stepford wife?"

When he explained the concept, I realized he was saying that he didn't want me to be a parrot, someone who was only going to reflect his opinions. He wanted me to think for myself and figure out what my convictions were and what I liked and disliked.

By living out Gothard's teachings, I had, without realizing it, become a version of a Stepford wife. I had conformed myself to a mold of what I thought women were supposed to be, which was agreeable, happy, and relentlessly encouraging. It's taken years for me to learn that it's okay to tell Jeremy I don't like green walls or I prefer he wear certain colognes and not others. Or that it's okay for me to get upset and discouraged. To have bad days. To not always be bubbly and cheery when Jeremy comes home.

That's real life. It's part of being human. I certainly want to grow in my joy and be as Christlike as I can, but I don't want to suppress myself and all my emotions like Gothard taught.

Yet his principles weren't the only barrier I had to overcome in learning to be my true self. Being on television also made this challenging for me. Other than a few moments of sadness, such as my grandmother's funeral, the show was overwhelmingly positive. We were supposed to be happy as we did things like play games, go on trips, or talk about our relationships.

The positive nature of the show affected my personal life. I was constantly worried that someone would recognize me and see me in a moment of weakness or discouragement. So I was always aware of my facial expressions in public, especially my smile. Even if I wasn't being filmed, I assumed someone was watching me and wanted to see me as they saw me on the show.

I'll never forget being at a restaurant in Laredo and finding glass in my meal. Instead of asking to see the manager, or even asking for another meal, I acted like everything was fine. I smiled and said it was no big deal. That's a small example of an attitude I carried with me and struggle with to this day. I assume that I must be happy and see everything in a positive light, even if there's glass in my food.

I also remember that whenever Jeremy and I played tennis or darts during that first year of marriage, I spent the whole game encouraging him and telling him he was doing amazing. I'd say over and over that he was better than me, even if I had just won the game. When I responded this way, I was reinforcing the belief that my life was a performance. Fortunately, Jeremy didn't want me to respond like that. He wanted me to be happy that I won. He would say, "Jing, I did horrible. You just beat me. It's okay to tell me that."

Along with my inexperience making friends and the performance mindset I took with me to church and home, I also struggled with one-on-one conversations because of the Gothard-inspired bubble in which I grew up. It had shielded me from anyone with different thoughts or opinions from my own—including Christians who didn't follow Gothard's principles.

If I had to steer clear of other Christians, you can imagine how little I interacted with people who did not believe in God or follow the Bible. I thought they could taint me spiritually and corrupt my mind. Too much friendship with the world could cause me to walk away from the Christian faith. I learned James 4:4, which says, "Do you not know that friendship with the world is enmity with God?

Therefore whoever wishes to be a friend of the world makes himself an enemy of God."

This lack of interaction with the world made it hard for me to understand why anyone would do things a different way than I did. If someone listened to music I didn't listen to, dressed in ways I never would, wore earrings in places I wouldn't, dyed their hair pink, or ate food I would never eat, I thought their decisions were not only wrong but also weird. Of course, there's a lot of irony in what I'm saying, especially for everyone who watched the Duggars on TV and thought we lived odd lives. But when you live in a community as insulated and isolated as mine was, you assume the way you live is normal and right.

In Laredo, I didn't know anyone who'd grown up exactly like I did. No one at Jeremy's church was from the IBLP world. They were the kind of Christians I hadn't interacted with much. They didn't grow up with the same convictions I did. And even though I was gradually changing my convictions, I still was having a hard time interacting with people whose lives and backgrounds were unfamiliar to me. My first year of marriage was the first time I formed friendships with people I wasn't related to, people who were not like me in many ways. And because I had little experience with people like that, I experienced a lot of anxiety talking to the sweet, kind, Christlike people I met in Jeremy's church.

## LEARNING HOW TO LOVE OTHERS

In Laredo, I didn't understand how to love others the way God loved me. I had no clue how to obey the second part of the Great Commandment, which is to love your neighbor as yourself (Matthew 22:35-40).

Part of my education in reading the Bible the right way was learning to ask questions of the text. The obvious questions for these verses are, *How do I love God and others?* and *What does that look like?* Thankfully, the answers are found all over the Bible.

I think the simplest definition of *love* is found in 1 John 4:16. "God is love, and whoever abides in love abides in God, and God abides in him." God doesn't only express love. He is love! It's who He is. So when God acts, we see love on display. And what is God's greatest expression of love? I found that answer in the Bible's most famous verse: John 3:16.

God's Son is, of course, Jesus Christ. He is truly God and truly man. When I was younger, I never thought about what Jesus was doing before He came to earth. He was with the Father in heaven, ruling over all creation, enjoying the constant praise and adoration of the angels. He gave that up to come to earth and become a man— and not just a man but a helpless baby. He lived in a small town in an outpost of the Roman Empire, far from any influence or power. For thirty years, He lived in obscurity. For three and a half years, He preached the gospel and ministered to the sick and poor. At the end of His ministry, He was arrested, charged with blasphemy, mocked, spit on, nailed to a cross, and crucified.

And that wasn't even the worst part. While He hung on that tree, God punished Him for the sins of the world. Jesus was innocent. He hadn't sinned once during His thirty-three years on earth. He was the only man in history ever to do that. His pure life made Him the perfect substitute for me and you. The suffering Jesus endured that day is unimaginable. For a few hours, Jesus became sin: "He made him to be sin who knew no sin, so that in him we might become the righteousness of God" (2 Corinthians 5:21). This verse, and so many others, tell me that people can become as righteous as Jesus because of what He did on the cross. How? It's actually quite simple: "Believe in the Lord Jesus, and you will be saved" (Acts 16:31).

By coming to earth, resisting all temptations to sin, suffering unimaginable hate from creatures He had formed in their mother's womb (Psalm 139:13), facing the holy wrath of His own Father, dying, and then rising again, Jesus made a way for us to be saved, go to heaven, and live with Him forever. All we have to do is believe. That's the best news I have ever heard!

What does any of this have to do with my social anxiety in Laredo? Everything! Jesus' life, death, and resurrection show me exactly what it looks like to love someone. Love is self-sacrifice. It is others-focused. It is giving all of yourself for the good of others. That's what Jesus did.

But that's not what I was doing in Laredo. I was thinking mostly about myself and worrying about how I was coming across. I was focusing on my appearance, my words, and my reputation. When I was having brunch with that young lady, I wasn't thinking of her. I wasn't giving all of myself to her. I was holding back. When I broke down in tears at my friend's home, I was overwhelmed because my focus was inward. Love turns it outward.

If love is giving all of yourself for the good of others, that doesn't just mean your strengths. It also means your weaknesses. I used to think the best thing I could do was be happy and agreeable all the time. I don't think like that anymore. Now I see that the best thing I can do for others is to be honest, vulnerable, and self-giving. At that brunch, I wish I had told my sweet, kind friend that I was struggling. I wish I had told her how little I knew and how much I wanted to learn about loving God, loving others, being a pastor's wife, and living in Laredo. I'm sure she would have given me wonderful advice.

I'm sure she would have shared much more about herself. We probably would have prayed together. I know our relationship would have been stronger for it. Instead, I smiled, ate my food, made small talk, and thought only of myself. I did not love her the way Jesus loves me. He gave all of Himself for me. I could have given part of myself for my friend.

Jeremy and I left Laredo for California a few years later, and I'll never forget what a longtime member of the church said to me on our last Sunday. She told me that she was going to miss me and that she regretted that she hadn't gotten to know me better. She said it seemed like I had kept people in the church at a distance, and she wished I hadn't. She was right. While I'm grateful that by the time we left, I had made some friends, dear people I miss to this day, I wish I had opened more of my heart to them. I had not let a lot of cherished people into my life, and my life was poorer because of it.

I don't know if I'll ever be completely free of my social anxiety until I go to heaven. Those habits of performance are hard to break. The fear of saying the wrong thing and embarrassing myself or my family may always be a struggle. And I still have a lot of catching up to do when it comes to interacting with people who think differently than I do. But by God's grace, the social anxiety does not control me like it did that first year of marriage. I am now seeking to focus my relationships around love. It is my desire to pursue a self-giving care for others that is marked by the kind of love described in 1 Corinthians 13: "Love is patient and kind; love does not envy or boast; it is not arrogant or rude. It does not insist on its own way; it is not irritable or resentful; it does not rejoice at wrongdoing, but rejoices with the truth. Love bears all things, believes all things, hopes all things, endures all things" (vv. 4–7).

Love does not seek its own benefit. That's what I was missing. But now I see that a self-giving love, instead of a self-protecting performance, not only causes others to flourish but also frees me from so many burdens. Love—God's love for me and my love for Him and others—casts those burdens aside.

# CHAPTER 10

# Laying Down My Burdens

*Not long after* Jeremy and I moved to California in 2019, we met Joey and Kinsey Mejia. The Mejias are about as Los Angeles as it gets. Joey grew up in Venice, LA's famous beach town known for its street art, skate parks, basketball courts, outdoor gyms, and colorfully dressed residents. Before his current job at the Master's Seminary, Joey was an accomplished hairstylist in Beverly Hills (he once cut Paul McCartney's hair). He worked as a DJ on a rock and roll station. His DJ name was LAJoey. And he sold clothes for Armani. Kinsey grew up in the mountains just outside LA. She was in a bluegrass band with her siblings, and her father worked for the Walt Disney Company.

If you met Jeremy and me and then Joey and Kinsey, you wouldn't think we had much in common. We not only come from different backgrounds we also have different perspectives on music, clothes, sports, and a wide range of other issues. Kinsey has tattoos and a nose ring. When I was a teenager, I would have thought it bizarre, even immoral, for a Christian to have either. Joey wears T-shirts with band names on them. Yet these differences have not kept us from becoming friends with and serving alongside the Mejias at our church. We may not see eye to eye about everything, but we do agree on the most important issues.

Since we moved to Los Angeles three years ago, I've met dozens of people like the Mejias. Most don't dress like us, talk like us, or share our interests or hobbies. At our church, there are nearly as many perspectives as there are people. On Sunday mornings, some men wear suits and ties while others show up in shorts and T-shirts. There are as many women wearing pants as skirts. There is a full orchestra in the main service, and we primarily sing hymns. In the college ministry where Jeremy and I serve, a full band with drums and electric guitars plays a range of worship songs. The pastors don't talk about an umbrella of authority. They don't encourage courting and discourage dating. They'd say that God, in His kind providence, uses a variety of means to bring a man and woman together for marriage.

Some congregants work in the entertainment industry, while others never watch movies. There are big families. Small families. Stay-at-home moms and women with careers. It's a large church with all the variety that comes from living in one of the biggest cities in the world. But we are incredibly united in our perspective on what matters most.

Members at our church share my love for the Bible. On a typical Sunday, I'll hear two sermons (if neither of my girls are under the weather, which is a big *if* for a four- and two-year-old). Each message is between fifty and sixty minutes in length. When our pastor preaches, he simply explains what the Bible means. He doesn't tell funny jokes or stories. He doesn't share his opinion. He describes what the Bible says, what it means, and how it can change anyone's life. And the people of our church submit to everything the Bible teaches, even if that puts them out of step with the broader culture.

I also know my church family wants to glorify God with everything they do. At Calvary, Jesus Christ bought them "with a price" as 1 Corinthians 6:20 says, so they want to do what the rest of the verse says: "glorify God in your body." Those who glorify God make His name well-known. They give God a good reputation and point to His fame, power, and character. Their changed lives show the world that God exists, that He is powerful, and that He is involved in the lives of His people.

The members of Grace Church share a desire to do that by telling a lost and dying world about Christ, working with excellence and integrity at their jobs, caring for others with their words and actions, and loving God with all their soul, strength, and mind (Luke 10:27). That love for God is probably the thing that most unites us as a church. We share a common love for God "because he first loved us" (1 John 4:19).

My current pastor has been preaching through the Bible, verse by verse, for more than fifty years. He's spent nearly half that time preaching from the four Gospels—Matthew, Mark, Luke, and John—looking at the life and teaching of Jesus Christ. He's even preached through the Gospel of John twice. This hasn't bored the church members though. Far from it. Because everyone loves Jesus, they want to spend as much time with Him as they can. There's unity around that love. Since we share a common love for Christ, the other issues are not as big a deal. There truly is far more that unites us than divides us.

Being at my current church has changed how I think about Christians who are different from me. The churches I grew up in did not have the same diversity, so I learned to see all Christians the same way. Now I understand what all Christians have in common and what they can have different perspectives on.

## UNITY VERSUS UNIFORMITY

Though there are about the same number of people at Grace Church every Sunday as there were at each of the IBLP conferences I attended, the crowds could not look more different. While people dress in a variety of ways at Grace Church, they were dressed mostly the same at the IBLP conferences. Women wore skirts from the time they arrived on the Big Sandy campus until the conference ended.

Walk across our church campus each Sunday and you'll hear a variety of greetings—a lot of them in different languages. At Big Sandy, greetings were all positive and encouraging. Ask someone how they were doing, and they would smile and say, "Doing well." There was even a season of life when Bill Gothard encouraged everyone to "give the perfect greeting," which involved responding to the question "how are you doing" with as big a smile as possible and the words "I'm rejoicing." I remember constantly hearing that greeting when I walked down the halls or interacted with someone at the IBLP headquarters one summer.

What I didn't understand then is that unity does not mean uniformity. The Bible allows for differences. It doesn't always tell you what to do. It doesn't say whether you should order beef, chicken, or pork. It doesn't tell you which house to buy or what shoes to wear. It doesn't even tell you which job to take or spouse to marry or whether you should marry at all. In those areas and so many others, Christians have the freedom to make their own decisions (as long as they aren't disobeying a direct command from the Bible). Sometimes those decisions may be different from another Christian's decisions—and the Bible says that's okay.

A good example of that is Romans 14. I read this chapter more than once as a kid, but I didn't understand what it was saying and how helpful it was until recently. This chapter has become so important to me. It's really shaped how I live. I want to share a little about this section of the Bible so that you can see why it matters so much for me and so many Christians who want to honor God. In this chapter, the apostle Paul talks to Christians who disagree about whether or not they should eat meat. The disagreement is messy.

Some people are so sure they shouldn't eat meat because it used to be offered to false gods. Other Christians don't think it's a big deal. That argument sounds so much like arguments I used to hear about clothes, music, and, yes, even food. So who was right? Paul said both were. Here are the first four verses of that chapter:

> As for the one who is weak in faith, welcome him, but not to quarrel over opinions. One person believes he may eat anything, while the weak person eats only vegetables. Let not the one who eats despise the one who abstains, and let not the one who abstains pass judgment on the one who eats, for God has welcomed him. Who are you to pass judgment on the servant of another? It is before his own master that he stands or falls. And he will be upheld, for the Lord is able to make him stand.

I'm amazed at the Bible's wisdom. In this chapter, it gives Christians the freedom to eat or not eat the meat because "the kingdom of God is not a matter of eating and drinking but of righteousness and peace and joy in the Holy Spirit" (v. 17). In other words, food isn't that big of a deal. It's not a priority in God's kingdom. It's not nearly as important as righteousness, peace, and joy. If someone has those three things, then it doesn't matter what kind of food they are eating or where that food came from. They are, as verse 18 says, "acceptable to God and approved by men."

## CHRISTIAN LIBERTY VERSUS RULES

Romans 14 and 1 Corinthians 8 are two of the main places where the Bible talks about Christian liberty. That's the idea that Christians have freedom to decide how to live, what to do, and even what to believe as long as those beliefs don't disagree with the Bible's essential truths about God, salvation, and Scripture. I didn't learn much about Christian liberty when I was younger.

I didn't realize that when I was judging other women for wearing pants, I was committing the same mistake as the Christians who didn't eat meat. I didn't know that when I assumed someone had a spirit of rebellion because they listened to music with drums, I was judging that believer for something God's Word did not condemn. I had no idea that I was being stricter than the Bible.

I recently came across a famous quote that is often falsely attributed to Saint Augustine but can most likely be traced back to a seventeenth-century Catholic source. Regardless of who originally penned these words, I think the quote gives a helpful perspective on how to have unity and differences among Christians. "In essentials, unity; in non-essentials, liberty; in all things, charity."[1] We unite around the gospel, we give freedom for differences of opinions on lots of other issues, and we seek—at all times—to love people.

That is a perspective I've had to learn. I've had to take a hard look at all the convictions I used to think were absolute necessities for all Christians and disentangle my essential convictions from the nonessential ones.

Something that made this process of disentangling a little easier was figuring out the differences between the Old and New Testaments. Growing up, I thought I had to obey everything the Bible commanded—whether it came from the Old or New Testament. Bill Gothard often referenced verses from Deuteronomy or Leviticus and said that Christians had to obey the command in those verses. This included commands about eating pork or certain kinds of seafood. It also included a lot of commands about clothes. There were specific orders for how far someone could walk, or what was considered work, on the Sabbath.

Jesus freed us from those commands. But we are still required to love God and others, just like the book of Deuteronomy says. Chapter 6, verses 4–5 say, "Hear, O Israel: The LORD our God, the LORD is one. You shall love the LORD your God with all your heart and with all your soul and with all your might." And Leviticus 19:18 says, "you shall love your neighbor as yourself." Now that I know the truth, that Jesus sets me free from those ceremonial laws, obedience has become less of a burden, and it's helped me be gracious toward others who have different convictions. It's also made me love Jesus so much. I can't keep all those Old Testament laws on my own. But Jesus ensured I wouldn't have to.

Why do pastors like Gothard have so many rules? Why do they teach that all Christians should dress the same, consume the same music and media, vote the same, and talk the same? Why did he even create rules about what food Christians are supposed to eat when the Bible clearly says, "the kingdom of God is not a matter of eating and drinking" (Romans 14:17), and Christians are not supposed to judge others for what they eat?

I think he did that because uncertainty can be unsettling. Rules are easier than liberty. They give a sense of certainty. They remove doubts and questions. Knowing exactly what to say and what to do in any situation to perfectly please God is an incredibly attractive idea. It certainly was for me, since I struggled with doubt and fear. Gothard's rules gave me certainty.

All those rules may have told me what to believe, but they didn't teach me how to think. Critical thinking was not important as I was growing up because what was there to think critically about? There was a right and a wrong way to do everything. Gothard apparently had figured all that out. All I had to do was follow his seven principles.

By far the most common extrabiblical source for Gothard's

rules was personal experience. It's called truth by analogy. Here's an example from one of Gothard's seminars. After arguing that sins are passed from one generation to the next, he used the following story to prove that is true. He described a young couple from California who adopted a girl. Not long after they became her parents, they started to notice problems. The baby didn't look at them with love. Instead, the baby had a cold, even hateful look in her eyes when she was looking at them. (I'm not sure I've ever seen a newborn with hate in its eyes, so I don't know what that would look like, but evidently it happened to this couple.) To fix the issue, the couple had to remember what Gothard had taught them about the sins of the fathers being passed on to the next generation. The couple figured that there must be some serious sins of hate and bitterness in this adopted girl's biological family. She would have certainly grown up to despise her adopted parents if they didn't recognize what was happening and ask God to take away the generational sin. The couple then told Gothard that their child was happy now because they had followed his steps for dealing with cross-generational sins.[2]

When I was a teenager, I definitely believed that sins could be passed from one generation to the next. A story like the one Gothard told would have been terrifying to me. It would have made me believe that there were all these hidden sins lurking in me that would come out not necessarily because of something I did but because of something my grandparents or great-grandparents did. That made me think I wasn't free to do certain things or go certain places because if I did, I might encounter a temptation that my family was particularly susceptible to. Then I would mess up and sin in the same way my previous family members had. Stories like this, and the principles at the heart of them, slowly chipped away at my

Christian freedom. They gave me, and I'm sure many others, rules that went beyond the Bible.

The slippery slope argument is another tactic Gothard used to bind the conscience of his audience. This is the idea that certain behaviors may not be bad in themselves, but they can lead to other behaviors that are immoral, sinful, or harmful. These behaviors are like gateway drugs—they lead to something far worse. One of the most common slippery slope arguments involves music. Gothard never used the Bible to preach against certain kinds of music, like rock and roll or rap. Instead, he used personal experience and the slippery slope argument. Here's an example.

Gothard and Jim Sammons, who taught the Financial Freedom Seminar at IBLP, would tell stories of men and women with credit card debt, mortgages, or car payments. When these people lost their businesses, when their marriage crumbled, or when their health took a turn for the worse, Gothard and Sammons would blame the debt. They would tell the audience that if they didn't stay out of debt, the same catastrophes would befall them.

Those kinds of arguments stifle debate. It's hard to argue with personal experience. They also make it easy for someone, like me, to judge others. When a personal experience becomes a black-and-white rule, it's natural to judge someone who is engaged in the behavior that you've been told can lead to a destructive outcome. I used to do that all the time.

What the Bible says about Christian liberty has freed me from that judgmentalism. The apostle Paul didn't say in Romans 14 that someone who ate meat offered to idols would one day start worshiping idols. He didn't see a slippery slope there. He saw only freedom. I've learned that if I have a conviction against something because it is spiritually unhelpful for me, that doesn't mean the same activity is spiritually unhelpful for someone else. That's the beauty of Christian liberty.

## FALSE TEACHERS VERSUS TRUE FREEDOM

In these last few chapters, I've traced the massive changes in my beliefs during the past three years: changes that have freed me from the legalism, fear, and man-made rules of my youth. In chapter 7, I described how the Lord freed me from a fear of Him by showing me that He is my heavenly Father. In chapter 8, I looked at how a true biblical understanding of love—one based on self-giving, not performance—freed me from my fear of people. And in this chapter, I've looked at Christian liberty. Christians can't have different convictions about the Bible, God, or salvation, but they can believe different things about all kinds of less-important issues. That has not only freed me from obedience to rules that are not in the Bible but also made me a less-judgmental person.

As I've come to understand the true freedom that's found in Christ, I've also realized that a teacher can preach the truth in public but value control and man-made rules in private. And that can be just as dangerous as a false teacher who tells people lies. I used to think the only dangerous teachers were those who convinced others that the Bible was a book of fairy tales and that God did not exist. Now I believe the far more dangerous false teachers are those who say they believe in God and the Bible but misrepresent Him and His Word. The Bible describes these false teachers as "having the appearance of godliness, but denying its power" (2 Timothy 3:5). They look like Christians. They talk like Christians. But they don't teach the truth. Instead, they teach a religion of their own creation. I've become convinced that Bill Gothard is one of those dangerous teachers.

If someone had told fifteen- or twenty-year-old Jinger that she would one day say something like that, she would have been horrified. She would have probably thought that meant she was going to one day abandon Christianity entirely. Back then, I thought Bill Gothard was a modern-day prophet. Before Jesus came to earth, God revealed Himself to His people through men like Noah, Moses, Elijah, Elisha, Isaiah, Jeremiah, and Jonah. A lot of books in the Old Testament are named after prophets because those books include many of the words God gave His people through those prophets. They were ordinary men with a supernatural message.

Bill Gothard was that kind of teacher to me. I thought his words were so powerful—and his message so unique and helpful—they were like a special revelation from God. Gothard never called himself a prophet, but when he said God had shown him a rhema or that he understood "the key" to the Christian life, he was setting himself up as the messenger of a special revelation from God.

Now I see that Gothard has nothing in common with the Old Testament prophets, who served only as mouthpieces of God. Instead, he seems to be more like the false teachers described throughout the New Testament in verses such as these:

- "For such men are false apostles, deceitful workmen, disguising themselves as apostles of Christ. And no wonder, for even Satan disguises himself as an angel of light. So it is no surprise if his servants, also, disguise themselves as servants of righteousness. Their end will correspond to their deeds" (2 Corinthians 11:13–15).
- "See to it that no one takes you captive by philosophy and empty deceit, according to human tradition, according to the elemental spirits of the world, and not according to Christ" (Colossians 2:8).

- "Beware of false prophets, who come to you in sheep's clothing but inwardly are ravenous wolves. You will recognize them by their fruits. Are grapes gathered from thornbushes, or figs from thistles? So, every healthy tree bears good fruit, but the diseased tree bears bad fruit. A healthy tree cannot bear bad fruit, nor can a diseased tree bear good fruit. Every tree that does not bear good fruit is cut down and thrown into the fire. Thus you will recognize them by their fruits" (Matthew 7:15–20).
- "I appeal to you, brothers, to watch out for those who cause divisions and create obstacles contrary to the doctrine that you have been taught; avoid them. For such persons do not serve our Lord Christ, but their own appetites, and by smooth talk and flattery they deceive the hearts of the naive" (Romans 16:17–18).

When Jesus said in Matthew 7 that you will know false teachers by their fruit, He was talking about the false teachers' actions. And when the apostle Paul said false teachers are slaves of their own appetites, he was talking about their desires. He was calling them selfish. They were the kind of people who would use their platform and influence over others for selfish gain and their own pleasure.

A few years ago, it became abundantly clear to me that this man I had always looked up to as a model Christian was, in fact, no better than the false teachers Jesus and Paul described. Gothard was not only teaching his own principles instead of Christ's but reportedly harming those closest to him.

# CHAPTER 11

# Did the Lifetime Guarantee Work?

*I'll never forget* that trip to the mall. My sisters and I weren't searching for anything in particular. We were doing what we typically did at the mall, browsing windows and bargain hunting. I can't remember exactly how old I was, probably close to twenty.

In one of the stores we browsed, we noticed a blond wig. It reminded us of a certain type of girl. We all tried it on and, for a few minutes, joked about being ready for headquarters.

By *headquarters*, we were of course referring to Hinsdale, Illinois, where Bill Gothard led the IBLP ministry. Why was it funny to say that a blond wig qualified us to work there? Because for years, people in our circles talked about how Bill Gothard liked to surround himself with pretty girls.

We all talked about how they were nicknamed "Gothard's girls." They ranged from teenagers to women in their midthirties. Most of them had long, blond hair, big smiles, and petite body types. Many came from single-parent homes, without a father or grandfather to guide and protect them. When they joined IBLP and met Gothard, they found someone who presented himself as the father they never had.

Other Gothard girls were daughters of parents who devoted their lives to following his principles. One girl said her parents thought of Bill Gothard as a modern-day apostle Paul.[1] Another talked about what an honor it was to be in his presence. This young woman's parents had decided to have more kids because of Gothard's seminars, so in a way, she owed her life to him.[2]

At the time, the joke in the mall didn't seem like that big of a deal. Everyone knew about Gothard's girls. For us, this wasn't more than an odd quirk of our little world. Now, after everything that's happened over the past ten years, I realize the joke wasn't funny. It's disturbing that an older man insisted on surrounding himself with young girls, some of whom were still minors. And he did so in the name of service to God.

Those poor girls. They had no idea what they were getting into.

Most of Gothard's girls first crossed paths with their hero at IBLP events. One recalled meeting him at a seminar in Knoxville, Tennessee. She said, "It was something you dreamed about—meeting Bill Gothard in the flesh. It was like the president of the United States tapping you on the shoulder. You don't expect it. In our world, the conservative, homeschool world, he was everything. There were hundreds of people there waiting to touch the hem of his garment."[3]

Gothard would compliment these young girls' "bright countenance." He would smile and say something nice about their outfits or demeanor. He would make them feel special, set apart from the hundreds of girls at the conference.

I remember one time watching him treat a girl this way at an IBLP conference. I was in a hallway that Gothard was walking through. He nodded his head and smiled at everyone as he passed. But when he saw this particular girl, he stopped, and compliments gushed out of him. He told her she had a radiant countenance. He told her how much he appreciated her smile. I thought this was completely normal. He had said nice things to me from time to time. It was always a great honor to get such encouraging feedback from Gothard. I had even sent him thank-you letters after visits to headquarters or IBLP conferences. I thanked him for taking the time to speak with me and shared that I owed my life to him as the sixth Duggar kid. If my parents had decided to stop having children when most Americans did, I wouldn't exist.

Even though I had several interactions with Gothard through the years, I never experienced what a lot of Gothard's girls did. With them, he would insist that God had a special plan for their lives. Then, as many of these girls testified later, he would ask them to have a private conversation with him, where he would insist they join the team at the IBLP headquarters. At an event in Indianapolis, he told a girl he'd just met he wanted her to come with him that night to Chicago.[4] This was an incredible honor for these young ladies. For most of them, it was a dream come true. Living and working in Chicago, near Gothard, was a sign of God's favor and blessing.

IBLP had offices around the country, and a few overseas, but since the 1970s, the ministry's headquarters were just outside Chicago. They had a series of buildings, including an old hotel they'd converted into dormitories. That's where these young ladies lived. Many were too young to be paid, so they would spend a few months or even a year "volunteering." Some would prepare meals for the staff. Others would work in the print shop and process the mail or clean and organize files. Most of them would help organize and lead Gothard's programs, including the annual conferences and Journey to the Heart. He would even take them on his ministry trips overseas.

It was the kind of work outside the home that was forbidden among IBLP families. There was something deeply ironic and hypocritical about all the young ladies staffing the organization's national offices. They were only allowed to work outside the home at the center of the movement that forbade them from working outside the home. Though interactions with the opposite sex were heavily regulated (the young ladies and men were not allowed to speak with one another in the lobby of IBLP headquarters), these young women could spend plenty of time alone with Gothard.

Former Gothard girls have described late-night conversations with this father figure. After the IBLP staff would leave for the day, Gothard—who often stayed late because he did not have a wife or children to go home to—would ask one of the young ladies to come see him. At first, the two would only talk. After a while, Gothard would rub the women's feet and hold their hands, both of which were strictly forbidden between a man and woman who were not married. A lot of Gothard's girls have said that Gothard would touch them inappropriately or engage in explicitly sexual activity. Ten of those ladies filed a lawsuit against Gothard in 2016. I don't want to describe all the awful things they accused him of. You can read about them in a *Washington Post* article from 2016.[5] But if true, Gothard should be permanently disqualified from ministry.

## GRACE RECOVERED

Allegations against Gothard started to surface in 2012, four years before the lawsuit, on a website called Recovering Grace. It was run by former IBLP members who had negative experiences with Gothard's teaching or claimed to be abused by him. The website says they started Recovering Grace "with a desire to expose the destructive effects of the teachings of Bill Gothard and the organizations he founded, that generations of former followers might find understanding, hope, and healing."[6]

I remember hearing about Recovering Grace when it launched.

I was a teenager at the time—still deeply committed to Gothard's teaching—so I was sure the people running the website were lying. I thought they were probably agents of Satan, sent to destroy Gothard and his teaching because he was anointed by God to bring sanity and truth back into our culture.

One year, Recovering Grace rented a billboard in Nashville, right next to the campus where I and hundreds of others were gathering for the annual ATI conference. The billboard took a clever approach to reaching people like me. In big, bold letters it said, "Welcome ATI Families," then it gave the website address for Recovering Grace. They were trying to get attendees to go to their website. I did not go to their website because I was horrified by the billboard. I shook my head in pity at the people behind the message. They had rejected Gothard's seminars. Trying to destroy such wonderful teaching was far worse than never hearing it at all. I thought, *They just don't know.* I felt the kind of self-righteous pity that looks more like self-satisfaction. I was confident they were wrong about Gothard and his principles.

Two years after Recovering Grace began posting stories of abuse, the number of accusers had grown so much they were impossible to ignore. More than thirty women had come forward. The IBLP board of directors had no choice but to listen to the accusations against Gothard. They launched an internal investigation and put him on administrative leave. He offered to step down, but the board unanimously refused to accept his resignation. When Gothard submitted his resignation a second time on March 5, 2014, the board accepted it.[7] Three months later, they insisted that "no criminal activity has been discovered" during the investigation. However, they did call Gothard's actions "inappropriate."[8] At the time of his resignation, they had not talked to any of the more than thirty women who accused Gothard of sexual misconduct.[9]

## MORE ACCUSATIONS

This 2016 lawsuit wasn't the first time Gothard was accused of wicked, predatory behavior by a young lady involved with IBLP. In the late 1970s, years before most of these women were born, Bill Gothard's brother Steve was working at a retreat center the organization ran in Michigan. Steve had multiple affairs with female staffers. Bill knew about his brother's immoral behavior, but, according to staff at the retreat center, he did nothing about it.[10] When Steve's abuse went public in 1980, so did Bill's inaction. Board members and other leaders at IBLP forced Gothard to resign. Yet he was reinstated in just a few weeks. The reasons behind the dismissal and quick reinstatement are lost to history. Investigations have tried to figure out why Gothard was so quickly reinstated, but there is no documented explanation for why he became president again so soon. What is clear is that from that point on, his control over the organization was stronger than ever.[11]

Gothard never admitted to doing anything wrong during the 1980 case beyond "'defrauding' several women" and mishandling the situation with his brother.[12] But thirty-six years later, he did confess to inappropriate behavior toward the women who were suing him. An undated letter from Gothard that one of the women showed the court during the 2016 lawsuit read: "I was very wrong in holding hands, giving hugs, and touching their hair and feet. I was also wrong in making statements that caused emotional turmoil and confusion." The letter also described what he did as "sin."[13]

The court did not convict Gothard, and the lawsuit was dropped in 2018. The ten plaintiffs didn't see the point in continuing because the statute of limitations made it impossible for Gothard to be convicted.[14] But he did lose his ministry.

When I heard about Bill Gothard's resignation, I was, of

course, stunned. I had just started to figure out that the faith of my youth was incomplete. I was in the middle of those conversations with Ben, Jessa, and the Seewalds that would guide me toward a richer, God-centered view of Scripture and the Christian life. I still had a high view of Gothard, but I was starting to question what I'd always been taught. I knew I could no longer focus exclusively on the ministry of one man. Here's what I wrote in my journal at the time:

> Today, we are in Big Sandy for the family conference. It is a different conference this year with Mr. Gothard not here. God is good and many people continue to come. I believe that it's an even greater awakening to the importance of not following a man but looking only to Jesus.

A decade after Gothard resigned from IBLP, he still insists that many of the charges against him are false, even publicly denying wrongdoing on his website.

> After 50 years of giving seminars on Basic Youth Conflicts in major cities across America, and in other nations, with over two and a half million attending, a website was established with the stated purpose of destroying me and the ministry. One of the founders of the website wrote, "As long as Bill Gothard is at the helm, nothing will change."
>
> The founders of this website recruited young women who had been part of the ministry twenty years earlier and convinced them that I had "sexually harassed" them. These same women had written marvelous letters of gratefulness to me during those 20 years, thanking me for "being their best friend," "bringing about the turning point" in their lives, and "giving the help and

encouragement" that they will always remember. There was never a hint of harassment because there was none.[15]

And Gothard hasn't stopped working. He regularly publishes books, articles, and curriculums with the same health and wealth message he's always preached. He credits his good works as the cause of God's blessing and the secrets that God has revealed to him in recent years as the cause of his successful Christian life. Everything, even his relationship with God, is still about his success.[16]

Gothard insists he should still be in charge of IBLP. The leadership at the organization have decided he is not above reproach, but he is still a valuable Bible teacher. That's why his resources and profile are still available on their website. Meanwhile, dozens of women have charged him with sexual harassment.[17] The sheer number of women is overwhelming, and I think their testimonies are too consistent to deny.

## IBLP CULTURE AND SEXUALITY

In light of these accusations, I want to share how IBLP approached the issue of sexuality and created an unhealthy culture for men and women. I see three major problems with their approach.

### An Unbiblical View of Sex

First, I don't believe IBLP's view of sex is biblical. The Bible teaches that intimacy within marriage is not only acceptable, it's good. It's a gift. Hebrews 13:4 says, "Let marriage be held in honor among all, and let the marriage bed be undefiled, for God will judge the sexually immoral and adulterous." Young people need someone who will help them understand that.

I worry that many young men and women who learn Gothard's principles are not learning what the Bible actually says about sex and marriage. Because they are sheltered from the topic, they see sex as taboo, dangerous, and embarrassing. When that happens, when sexuality becomes the great enemy, it stirs feelings of shame. Making the issue of sex both so powerful that it should be totally avoided and so taboo that it is embarrassing, does not help anyone. In fact, it often encourages young people to hide their desires and live double lives. Sadly, in my experience, this is common.

## An Unbiblical View of Marriage

Second, I don't think Gothard's views encouraged a healthy treatment of women. Wives were pressured to smile and be upbeat at all times, no matter what they were feeling inside. And they were told to not have any expectations of their husbands.

Here's one example of a time Gothard encouraged a wife to do just that:

> Here's a woman that has dinner all ready for her husband—six thirty. But no husband. Seven o'clock. Still no husband. Seven thirty. Finally, quarter of eight, the husband comes in. And by that time, she's hot and the food is cold. And nothing tastes good that night because she said, "He should've called me ahead of time if he's gonna be late. He knows he's supposed to call me!" So nothing tastes good that night. So then let's say, the next day, that she follows this very important step: that evening, six thirty no husband. Seven, seven thirty, still no husband. Finally, quarter of eight, the husband comes in and when he comes in, she is thrilled to see him because she wasn't expecting him at all! Now, I guarantee that he's gonna be aware of her new attitude. In fact, at first he'll wonder what she wants and then he'll wonder how

long it's gonna last and when he sees that attitude lasting, then God will begin to do a work in his life. Again, wives, and anyone under authority, that matter of gratefulness is more powerful, more important than you realize.[18]

I used to think stories like this were helpful. Now I think they can be dangerous—and hurt a lot of women. Such stories can make them think it's their job, and theirs alone, to keep the marriage together. In this instance, Gothard was telling wives not to communicate their expectations with their husbands. He was telling them to be passive. Simultaneously, he was saying that the husband bore no responsibility to keep his word and be faithful to his family. The husband was given free rein to behave how he wanted and should only be encouraged by his wife.

I really believe this led to a culture where men felt a lack of consequences for their actions. It's sad because true leadership is servant leadership. It is leadership that looks like Jesus, who served the church by giving up His life for her. If a man truly wants to lead his wife, he must selflessly serve her by considering her needs and caring for her well-being. This is how Jesus cares for His bride, the church: "Husbands, love your wives, as Christ loved the church and gave himself up for her" (Ephesians 5:25).

I'm grateful that Jeremy models that Christlike love in our marriage. He understands his God-given responsibility to me and our children. And he does not expect me to be cheerful and put-together all the time. He doesn't make me think it's my responsibility to care for his every need and not ask him to help around the house or serve in any way. As I said previously, he's often encouraged me to express my feelings and opinions. That's been hard for me at times. Our marriage has involved a process of me disentangling the truth—that I should respect, love, and honor Jeremy—from the lie that I, and I alone, am responsible for the health and longevity of our marriage.

## An Unbiblical Legalism

Third, I have concerns about IBLP's legalistic approach. While the Bible says the true evidence of righteousness is the presence of the Holy Spirit and the fruit He provides—"love, joy, peace, patience, kindness, goodness, faithfulness, gentleness, self-control" (Galatians 5:22–23)—a legalist says the true evidence of righteousness is obeying man-made rules. In Gothard's world, those rules were wearing the right clothes, listening to the right music, eating the right food, and avoiding wrong activities.

Following man-made rules has the appearance of being righteous. But they have no power to actually transform a life. It's just like Jesus told the hypocrites in Matthew 23:5: "They do all their deeds to be seen by others," he warned. "Woe to you, scribes and Pharisees, hypocrites! For you clean the outside of the cup and the plate, but inside they are full of greed and self-indulgence" (v. 25). That's a powerful picture.

True righteous living comes from a heart that has been transformed. But Gothard missed this. And the consequences were devastating. He told us what clothes we had to wear, what our homes had to look like, and how long our hair needed to be. He gave us lists for how to earn God's favor financially, physically, and relationally. He had the keys to success in the kingdom of God. Or so he thought. But he couldn't tell us how to truly live a life that honored God because man-made principles are a cheap substitute for true religion. And for Gothard, when you add his personal hypocrisy with his unbiblical teaching, you get the picture of a man who resembles the religious leaders Jesus was speaking to.

I think the message Jesus had for the abusive religious leaders of

His day is the same message He has for Gothard. Obsessed with outward appearances and man-made rules, Gothard missed the whole point of following Jesus. Sure, he was able to convince himself and many of his hearers that they were godly because they followed his rules. But there was evidently no actual power in his life and, sadly, in the lives of many who followed him. The uncovering of hypocrisy shows that.

One of the hardest realities in my life is that my brother Josh very publicly displayed some of the same hypocrisy as Gothard. He used his platform, and even his job at the Family Research Council, to promote some of the same ideas Gothard taught. But while he looked the part in so many ways, the true Josh appears to be much different. He was living a lie. Even though he claimed to follow Jesus, his actions gave no evidence of a true love for the Lord, a heart changed by the gospel. Watching all the pain Josh's sin has caused not only shows me the danger of hypocrisy but also reveals that external religion, a life of performance, has nothing to do with following Jesus. Though I haven't seen or spoken to Josh in nearly two years, I still pray for him. I ask God to show Josh his desperate need for repentance. I want my brother to be genuine and honest about his sin and reject the hypocrisy that has been part of his life for so long. Only Jesus can save him. False religion and man-made rules never will.

Gothard's rules can't transform anyone. They couldn't even transform him. Only Jesus can do that. What Gothard and my brother Josh need is a new heart that only Jesus can give. That's what I need. That's what we all need. Without a new heart, all the outward religious behavior isn't going to please God.

The fall of Bill Gothard is profound evidence that a ministry built on man's efforts and external righteousness will crumble. During the 1980s, the heyday of IBLP, he was packing stadiums.

Tens of thousands were attending his seminars and IBLP was making millions of dollars from donations, seminars, and literature.[19] More than three decades later, the organization now runs only a couple events each year with a few thousand people. The budget has shrunk, with revenue being lost every year. Beyond that, the generation of those raised in the movement, young people like myself, are leaving in droves. They did not find true spirituality there, so they have left IBLP behind.

Time and truth go hand in hand. Given enough time, someone's true self is bound to come out. It can't stay hidden forever. When Gothard's true self was exposed, it disqualified his ministry. The teachings he promised would bring success and victory didn't. Not even for him. If the proof of effectiveness is in the product, then Gothard's life proves his principles don't work.

# CHAPTER 12

# My Post-Reality Show Life

*We got the* call on June 26, 2021, that TLC was canceling *Counting On.* When the call ended, I wrapped my arms around Jeremy and cried. Hard. So many emotions poured out of me that day.

I felt sad. Filming had been a constant in my life since I was around ten years old. When the show was on break and the crews didn't come around for a few months, I missed the energy and excitement of interacting with all the creative people. The producers worked with my family to come up with ideas for episodes. It was fun to think of creative ways to give audiences a glimpse into our day-to-day lives.

I didn't mind when the filming complicated my routine. At least once, a camera crew burst into my bedroom early in the morning, not knowing that I was still in bed (because no one could keep track of where all the Duggar kids were). As they set up for an interview or film session, I had to clear my throat or say an awkward hello to let them know I was hiding under the covers. They apologized sheepishly and scrambled to the door. If the cameras were rolling, I couldn't always read where I liked or walk down hallways at certain times because it would interfere with a shot. Maybe I had to come up with something to say during an interview or take a few crew members with me when I went on an errand.

Moments like that probably would have been annoying or embarrassing if I didn't have such great relationships with the crew.

Many had filmed our family through all ten seasons of *19 Kids and Counting*, then every episode of *Counting On*. All those years on television provided job security for the film crew, and they became lifelong friends for us. One crew member, Scott, started working on the show as a cameraman. He filmed me on day one, when I was just ten years old. After several years behind the camera, documenting some of the biggest moments of my family's life, he became a producer on the show in 2015. Scott was there for the early days of my relationship with Jeremy. He captured our wedding for the show. He even came along with Jeremy and me to Australia for our honeymoon. In fact, when we were trying to decide where to go for our honeymoon, we asked Scott for a recommendation. He said Australia because it was the only continent he'd never been to. So that's where we went. Having him and the rest of the crew in Australia with us didn't ruin our trip. They gave us space and privacy when we asked. They truly were the best part of filming both shows, and not seeing them on a regular basis is the saddest part of no longer producing episodes.

Alongside sadness that the show was ending, I felt grateful to have been a part of it. I had countless wonderful experiences thanks to the show. When the cameras were around, you never knew what the producers were going to suggest. Skydiving. Eating exotic foods. Traveling to another city. My parents couldn't have afforded to take the entire family across the country several times a year, much less overseas. There are dozens of places and cultures I wouldn't know anything about if not for the show.

Growing up on television taught me so much about production, content creation, and filming. I was allowed to share ideas with producers. I could recommend story lines and discussion topics.

I'm still surprised the show lasted as long as it did. In the early years, my family assumed the show would last no more than a season or two. It didn't seem possible that that many Americans would be interested in a family with our conservative values. Yet each year, TLC renewed the show. For most of my life, that wasn't a burden. But even though I enjoyed being part of the show, I was also glad it was ending. In fact, I felt immense relief on that day in June 2021.

For more than a year, Jeremy and I had felt it was time to step away—not only for ourselves but for our children, Felicity and Evangeline. We didn't want our daughters to grow up on TV. We wanted to raise them out of the public spotlight. At their age, they don't get to choose to be part of a television show. We didn't think it was fair to make that choice for them. For all the wonderful experiences I had on the show, there were also difficult parts I couldn't have imagined when I was ten years old. When I walk out the front door of my house in Los Angeles, there are sometimes photographers waiting to take pictures of me that they can sell to the tabloids. I wish this didn't happen, but I can't stop it. All I can do is smile, try to be polite, and go about my day.

Being on television, especially a show that celebrates conservative biblical values, also gives people license to criticize you for moral failures, big or small. In the case of my brother Josh, the fall has been even more devastating because he claimed to be a man of Christian conviction. The backlash against his actions has been, correctly, severe. Even if he weren't a public figure, he would still be in prison for his actions. But because millions know who Josh is, his sin gives Christ a bad name. Those who oppose Christianity can point to Josh as evidence that anyone who claims to walk with Jesus is a phony.

When I was younger, I didn't understand the possibility of all that criticism. I don't think anyone in my family did. We weren't familiar with celebrity culture and the way people both admire and criticize television and movie stars. My parents had the best intentions when they committed to the documentaries and then the show on TLC. They wanted to show the world a positive, wholesome family that put God at the center of their lives. It was impossible to predict how popular the show would become and everything that would go along with it, including how being on television can turn life into a performance. I think it's good for me to be away from that mindset.

Finally, I felt a mix of anticipation and excitement when TLC canceled *Counting On.* In many ways, the show's end was the last leg of a journey that ten-year-old me could not have dreamed would occupy so much of my life. I could hardly remember what it was like to not be on television. So many of life's big moments had happened on the show. I'd grown from a little girl to a young adult to a married woman to a mother. I'd gone from Arkansas, the only home I'd ever known, to Texas, and then to Los Angeles. I'd become a Christian, then a pastor's wife. So much of my identity was connected to the show. It had consumed much of my time and focus. Some weeks when I still lived in Arkansas, we would film almost every weekday. With the travel and interviews required to film *Counting On*, the show had a tendency to crowd out other interests and priorities. Although filming had slowed down since Jeremy and I moved to California, now that it was completely gone, there was going to be plenty of time added to the calendar. I was looking forward to the future.

## A GLIMPSE INTO MY LIFE TODAY

What does my life look like today?

These days my life is filled with relationships. Instead of talking to millions of people through a camera, I'm talking to one or two at a time in my living room. Many members of my family have visited from Arkansas. I love showing them around Los Angeles and taking them to our church. Jeremy's parents often visit from Pennsylvania. People I couldn't have imagined being friends with a decade ago now spend the night at my house. That includes musicians who stay at our house whenever they visit Los Angeles. They get a kick out of how unfamiliar I am with popular music. Pastors and Christian leaders come over for dinner and stay late into the night, filling our home with conversations about God and the Bible.

Since Jeremy and I serve in college ministry, hardly a week goes by that we don't have students in our home. Most of these young people have no idea who my family is. They don't expect my house to be perfectly clean or notice if my children cry. Instead, they sit on our couch and share their hopes and dreams, their problems and joys.

At first, this kind of honesty was hard for me to understand. When we lived in Laredo, Jeremy and I were once speaking with a pastor friend of ours. I was struck by his honesty and his willingness to be open with us. He wasn't afraid to talk about his weaknesses. It was an encouraging conversation. I realized that I needed to be more like our friend: honest, willing to ask for prayer. I'm learning that the church should be full of that kind of honesty. We are all broken, sinful, and in desperate need of grace. As Pauline Phillips said, "A church is not a museum for saints—it's a hospital for sinners."[1] Asking for help is not a sign of weakness. It's a sign of strength.

Not long ago, my friend Merilly Duncan, a godly woman at our church who is married to our college pastor, Austin, came over for a visit. At the time, I was going through a season of serious discouragement. Our daughter Evangeline was less than a year old, and I think I may have been struggling with postpartum depression. In the past, I would have smiled and told everyone I was fine while burying my weaknesses. But this time, I managed to share what I was feeling, and I'm so glad I did. Merilly was not only encouraging (and not at all surprised by what I was going through) but also able to share practical tips to help me navigate that season.

I still tend to keep my struggles to myself. I don't like to burden others with what I'm feeling. But I'm learning that in the body of Christ, the church, I'm serving others by sharing my life, even the messy parts. Honesty binds us together and brings the kind of unity the Bible talks about.

Though I would have always said church was important, and I attended every week, I didn't truly cherish the local church until I lived in Laredo, then Los Angeles. Today, my pastor's weekly teaching is life-giving, not soul-crushing. Each week I leave with a better understanding of what the Bible means and a bigger view of God's character.

One Sunday not too long ago, Austin Duncan preached a sermon titled "Are You Stricter than Jesus?"[2] The title alone was convicting. In Mark 9:38–42, Jesus' disciple John saw someone casting out demons in the name of Jesus and told this man to stop because he wasn't one of Jesus' disciples. John made up a rule: only Jesus' disciples could cast out demons. That might seem right. Why would anyone not connected to Jesus get to use His name to do something so powerful? But Jesus didn't agree with John's rule. He had no problem with this man casting out demons in His name. Likewise, Austin warned Christians not to come up with rules that aren't in the Bible. He told us not to believe we are following God when we are really following a man-made standard.

Today, I'm still trying to disentangle those man-made standards from what the Bible teaches. I still have feelings of guilt when I don't read the Bible as much as I think I should. Though I try to read every morning, that doesn't always happen. A child will wake up earlier than expected, or I will sleep a little longer than I planned. My mind is prone to wander while I read. I'm tempted to pick up my phone when I should be focused on the text. In those times, when guilt wants to rise in my soul and condemn me, I remind myself that the Bible doesn't tell me how much I'm supposed to read it. It does tell me to love it, understand it, and believe it. By not condemning myself when I miss a morning, I'm no longer being stricter than Jesus. The same applies to other areas, like clothes, entertainment, and relationships. The body of Christ is helping me untangle the man-made standards and embrace God's truth.

This season of life, one focused on investing in the church and continuing this lifelong project of disentangling my faith, is in many ways defined by our daughters. They are my number one priority. The days can sometimes be messy and exhausting. My house is rarely as clean as I'd like it to be, and there are lots of days I never make it out of the house or even out of sweats. Yet I know this is exactly where I'm supposed to be.

## WHAT I WANT MY DAUGHTERS TO KNOW

Being a parent has taught me many profound lessons about the Lord's love and care. I love my girls so much and will do anything to protect and provide for them. Yet as much as I love them, my love doesn't compare to God's great love for them. When thinking about God's love, I often go back to Matthew 7:7–11. Few passages of the Bible are more encouraging than this:

> Ask, and it will be given to you; seek, and you will find; knock, and it will be opened to you. For everyone who asks receives, and the one who seeks finds, and to the one who knocks it will be opened.

Or which one of you, if his son asks him for bread, will give him a stone? Or if he asks for a fish, will give him a serpent? If you then, who are evil, know how to give good gifts to your children, how much more will your Father who is in heaven give good things to those who ask him!

I want my daughters to know that God will generously love them.

I not only want to always be there for my children, loving and sacrificing for them, but I also want to help them put fear in its proper place. I want them to trust God. If they are going to live with more faith than fear, they need to have a right view of God. I want to help them learn who He is and why they should trust Him.

Not long ago, Felicity asked me, "Does God see everything I do?" I had to fight back tears. I probably asked my mom a few questions like that when I was four years old like Felicity. While I don't know exactly what my daughter was thinking at that moment, I know she was curious about what God is like and what that means for her. At that moment, I felt the weight of responsibility. I wanted to make sure my answer didn't cause my daughter to be afraid of God and forget that He is love (1 John 4:8). At the same time, God does see everything, and He hates sin. Try explaining that to a four-year-old! It's not always easy to explain big theological truths to children. But it's important if I want to be faithful to the truth and help my children avoid the same fear and misunderstanding that I used to experience.

In the coming years, when Felicity and Evangeline ask me and Jeremy questions like, "How powerful is God? Does He love me? Does He get mad at me when I disobey? Does He like me?" I pray we will point them to what the Bible says about God and encourage them to draw near to Him.

Over the past year, I've spent a lot of late nights at my computer writing this book. Many of those nights, one of the girls would wake up because of a bad dream. Evangeline—our two-year-old—likes to move around a lot, and sometimes she will wake herself up. She's even gotten her foot caught in the crib a few times. In those moments, I've needed to stop writing and start caring for my girls. There have been moments of complete exhaustion that have required all my strength and endurance. As Jeremy or I, or both of us, lay with our girls and comfort them, I try to think about God's care for me. Despite my weaknesses, He is patient with me. Through all the mistakes I've made, He's continued to love me. I want to model that patience and love with my girls. Right now, that means I have to be willing to be interrupted, even with writing deadlines, and I have to be willing to lose a lot of sleep! In the coming years, it will mean I'll have to listen more as my girls tell me about their fears and hopes, dreams and anxieties. And one day, it will mean I let go as they start their own families. No matter what stage my girls are in, I want them to know one thing: the love I have for them will never stop. And it can hardly compare to the love God has for them.

## HOW I HOLD ON TO JESUS

As I reflect on my journey over the past decade, part of me is amazed that I am holding tightly to the gospel of Jesus Christ. Many of my peers who grew up under Gothard's teaching, or another strict religious system, want nothing to do with Christianity. For years, they invested all their hopes in man-made rules. Despite all that, they still discovered, as I did, that those rules could never restrain their sinful hearts.

When they didn't experience the blessed life Gothard promised, when they struggled with purity, anxiety, and doubt, they questioned his rules. They saw the hypocrisy. They were close with people who said they loved Jesus but then behaved as if they didn't know Him. This tore their faith down to the studs, and they never built it back up with the truth. Instead, they abandoned all religion. There's a sense in which this is the easy route. It's less work to abandon the house once you've torn it down than to lay another foundation and build it again, brick by brick. I can imagine a world where I abandoned Christianity entirely and instead built a new life from my desires. But that didn't happen because Jesus saved me. His love compelled me to keep trusting Him. I wish my friends knew that same love.

Speaking of His people, Jesus said, "I give them eternal life, and they will never perish, and no one will snatch them out of my hand. My Father, who has given them to me, is greater than all, and no one is able to snatch them out of the Father's hand" (John 10:28–29). I follow Jesus today because He has placed me in His hand, and He will not let me go. He has set His love on me, and He has said, "I WILL NEVER DESERT YOU, NOR WILL I EVER FORSAKE YOU" (Hebrews 13:5 NASB1995). I cannot give up on Christianity because Christ will not give up on me.

Perhaps you are reading this book and you are not a Christian. Maybe you reject the strict, conservative religious community that raised you, and you picked up this book hoping I was going to tell you that I had turned my back on my faith. You were imagining a story of enlightenment: a religious girl raised to always wear skirts and never kiss boys became an atheist or agnostic and now believes the Bible is nothing more than a collection of fairy tales. Sorry to disappoint you. That's not my story.

My faith is as strong as it's ever been—not because Christianity tells me the right way to live or unlocks some "key to success" but because I can find no one more compelling, more lovely, more hopeful than Jesus.

When I look at the man-made rules I put so much hope in when I was young, I see only emptiness. More emptiness and hopelessness would have greeted me if I turned to the world, just as they've greeted so many who have gone down that path. There is only one place to turn for the kind of hope that never fails: Jesus Christ.

I can't leave Christianity because only there can I find Christ. He is worth it. If you've left man-made religion, don't replace it with a religion of your own choosing. Replace it with a person. Jesus. He is all that's left—and all I will ever need—at the end of my story of disentanglement.

# CHAPTER 13

# Disentangling Your Faith

*When Jeremy was* little—two or three years old—he found his dad's therapy putty and took it with him to bed. It was warm and fun to squeeze. Not long after he fell asleep, the putty somehow became tangled in his hair. As he slept, the cool air hardened the putty, molding it to his scalp. Jeremy woke up early the next morning and snuck into his parent's bedroom while it was still dark. As soon as his mother, Diana, hugged him, she could tell something was off.

The top of his head felt hard, like a giant scab. She jumped out of bed, turned on the light, and saw, to her horror, that a hard block of dry putty had become as much a part of Jeremy's head as his hair or scalp. She couldn't simply cut his hair off and remove the putty. That wouldn't detach it from his scalp. She needed to somehow loosen the putty, then slowly unthread it from her son's head. She used olive oil, pouring it on his head until the putty started to break apart. Then she spent an entire day, from five thirty in the morning until the evening, pulling small pieces of the putty off her son. The process was painstaking. It required gentleness to protect Jeremy's scalp. And it called for patience.

Diana first told me that story last year, not long after I started writing this book. My story of disentangling my faith reminded her of what it took to free Jeremy from the hardened putty. I love that analogy. Something precious—the head of her child—was attached to a lifeless piece of clay. The same could be said of my spiritual journey. I've spent the last decade disentangling something precious—the truth—from the errors that were attached to it.

In this final chapter, I want to talk to any of you who may need to disentangle your faith like I did. Maybe you were not influenced by Bill Gothard. Maybe you were. Maybe you grew up under teaching more harmful than Gothard's. Maybe you were even part of a cult led by an abusive, manipulative man who claimed to speak for God—or even to *be* a god. Whether you fit into any of those categories, or you're simply wondering if a leader you've always trusted is telling you the truth, I hope this chapter is helpful.

## SEEKING HUMILITY

For me, the journey from error to truth has been a humbling experience. I had to admit that much of what I'd always believed was not just inaccurate; it was unhelpful, even harmful. That wasn't easy. To be honest, it was terrifying. Maybe the hardest part was being willing to listen to the criticism of what I had previously believed.

I had always thought that the best path through life was under Gothard's teaching. Maybe you, too, have been convinced for years that the only way to please God is by following specific man-made rules from a particular teacher. God had to humble me so I could see that all my effort was not actually honoring God. You may be in a similar situation, ready to examine your convictions and compare them to Scripture. That process is well worth it. No matter who you are or where you come from, you need what I need—what we all need. That's humility.

Through this process, I've come to understand that humble people don't think too much of themselves, but they don't think too low of themselves either. Humble people know who they are, what they are good at, and what talents they do not have. Romans 12:3 provides a great description of a humble person: "For by the grace given to me I say to everyone among you not to think of himself more highly than he ought to think, but to think with sober judgment, each according to the measure of faith that God has assigned."

Ten years ago, I don't think I understood that. I thought I had life figured out. I assumed my beliefs were superior, regardless of whether I could find what I believed in the Bible. And I judged people who didn't live like me. Judgmentalism is a clear sign of pride. I still struggle with pride, and I always will. But I'm grateful for the humility God is working in me. He opened my eyes, as only He can, to see that I was thinking too highly of myself. He gave me undeserved grace. As James 4:6 says, "But he gives more grace. Therefore it says, 'God opposes the proud but gives grace to the humble.'"

Without God's help, it's tough to see our pride. In fact, I'd say it's impossible. If you and I are ever going to submit to God and His Word, we need to begin by asking for humility. That's a request I know God will grant. After all, Proverbs 11:2 says, "When pride comes, then comes disgrace, but with the humble is wisdom." And I know that if I ask for wisdom, God will give it to me. Ask God for wisdom. Ask Him to show you where you may need to change. No one can step out of a false religious system if they are unwilling to take that first step. That was what I had to do to begin my disentanglement journey.

## RECOGNIZING THE NEED FOR CHANGE

The second part of my journey was probably the most emotionally difficult to take. I had to recognize that change was necessary and be willing to admit that ideas I'd always believed were not true. Of course, no one likes to challenge their beliefs. It's unsettling. It fills life with uncertainty. It can feel like an earthquake is happening and you aren't sure what the ground is going to look like when the shaking stops.

So how did I know I had to go through this disentangling process? How did I figure out that my convictions had a mix of truth and error? First, I needed to take a close look at not just what Gothard was teaching but also how he was teaching it. When I did that, I realized he was using fear to manipulate and control me.

I recently came across an article on the front page of Bill Gothard's website titled "Why So Many Teens Join a Cult." Gothard gave five reasons this happens. First, "cults thrive on a passive mind." Second, they "appeal to the lusts of the flesh." Third, they "activate the fear of rejection." Fourth, they "instill lies in the gut brain of followers" (I think he's talking about a person's innermost thoughts and desires). And fifth, they "use guilt to deaden the conscience of their followers."[1]

When I read that, I was surprised because all those points are true of what he taught me, particularly the third and fifth points. Because the community surrounding him was so tight-knit, it became impossible to imagine life outside that world. The thought of losing my place in IBLP was frightening. And as Gothard talked about all the ways my actions could displease God and remove His blessing, he was activating a fear of God's punishment. He was using a fear of God to bring me back for more of Gothard's teaching. The only way to avoid God's punishment was to obey the basic principles.

I also understand now that when I was listening to a Gothard seminar, I was being given more and more reasons to feel guilty—as the fifth point suggests. His messages described all the ways I could fall short of God's standards. That instilled in me constant guilt. I wasn't measuring up, so I needed to listen to more seminars.

Gothard set up his teaching in a way that made me believe I couldn't navigate life the way God wanted me to without Gothard.

As you think about your spiritual life, ask yourself: Am I relying too much on the opinions of men? Is someone serving as my primary source of truth instead of the unchanging Word of God? If you come to that conclusion and are willing to change, you have taken a huge step on your own disentanglement journey.

Under the fifth point about cults on his website, Gothard said the way to keep teens from joining cults is to make sure they are getting private interpretations of the Bible: "The only way to freedom is for a cult member to get daily Rhemas from reading the Bible, memorize them, and quote them to God every night while going to sleep. During the night they will go down to his gut brain and cleanse it from false teachings. Then the verses will instruct his heart brain with wisdom (Psalm 16:7). His heart brain will control his head brain."[2]

This quote is from one of the many articles Gothard continues to post on his website. It's new material, but I see it as more of the same problematic ideas he's always taught. He is giving his readers more rules to follow. For that reason, I believe his solution is more likely to produce guilt than to keep a teenager from it. That's what happened to me. The more I tried to follow rules and failed, the more guilty I felt. As you've read this book, maybe you've realized that you, too, have been influenced by someone whose tactics were designed to produce fear, not freedom. If that's the case, I encourage you to study what the Bible says about the fear of God and what Jesus does with our guilt.

I'm not saying that if you are going to disentangle your faith, you have to stop listening to your pastors or teachers. That's not helpful, and it's not biblical. Talking about spiritual leaders, Hebrews 13:7 says, "Remember your leaders, those who spoke to you the word of God. Consider the outcome of their way of life, and imitate their faith." I always want to encourage Christians to support, love, and listen to their spiritual leaders. But as they do that, I also encourage them to compare what they are taught to the Bible.

There's a cool example of this in the Bible itself. The apostle Paul was teaching a group of people called the Bereans. The Bible calls these people "noble" because they didn't blindly accept everything Paul said as truth. They examined his teaching and compared it to the Bible (Acts 17:11). That's something all of us need to do.

If the people listening to Gothard had examined the Bible to make sure he was teaching the truth—if they hadn't been content to take Gothard's word for it—many would not have followed him. The same is true of any spiritual leader. If you want to be sure your leaders are teaching you truth, keep your Bible open and compare what they are telling you to what the Bible actually says.

A big part of my disentangling journey was asking what Gothard was using to motivate me. Fear? Threats? Guilt? Or love? Was he convincing me that the only solution to my problems was to follow his principles, or was he pointing to a solution beyond himself? A true leader recognizes that he is not the source of all wisdom. He sees himself as a conduit to the truth that existed long before he came into your life and will still exist long after he is out of your life. Gothard believes he is the source of truth, and I used to believe that I couldn't reach my full potential without his teaching. But the man I followed is a hypocrite who couldn't even follow his own rules. When I saw that, I realized something needed to change.

## FINDING THE RIGHT SOURCE OF AUTHORITY

The next step in the journey of disentangling God's truth from error is to find the right source of authority. In chapters 4 and 6, I talked about what the Bible is and what it is about. I said it comes from God. It has no mistakes. It is the beautiful story of how God created the earth, rules over it, and has redeemed it through Jesus. What I didn't do in those chapters that I'd like to do now, is explain *why* I believe the Bible is what it says it is: the words of the living God. Second Timothy 3:16 says, "All Scripture is breathed out by God and profitable for teaching, for reproof, for correction, and for training in righteousness." A lot of ink has been dedicated to this topic. Some people say the Bible is just a human book. Others say it comes from God. I can't write an entire book trying to convince you that the Bible is God's Word. Much smarter people than me have done that! But I can explain why the Bible is my authority and why I think it should be yours.

First, I trust the Bible because it has proven again and again to be historically accurate. There are hundreds of prophecies in the Old Testament. Those are predictions people made about what was going to happen in hundreds, if not thousands, of years. All of them came true. Every single one. That includes the prophecy that the Messiah would be born in a small town called Bethlehem (Micah 5:2). And the strange, specific prediction that the Messiah wouldn't break a single bone when He died on the cross (Numbers 9:12). If you take the time to read what the Bible says, you will discover all kinds of stories that can't be disproven.

Second, I trust the Bible because it has changed my life. Reading Scripture the right way has shaped me in profound ways. It's changed my perspective on fear, doubt, and pride. It humbles me, especially when it says I am a sinner, incapable of doing any good on my own. As Romans 7:18 says, "For I know that nothing good dwells in me, that is, in my flesh. For I have the desire to do what is right, but not the ability to carry it out." The Bible teaches me about what Jesus did. The Holy Spirit convicts me of sin and changes my attitude, desires, and motives. I trust the Bible because I have experienced profound change when I understand and believe it.

Third, I trust the Bible because of Jesus. The Holy Spirit has given me eyes to see that Jesus is who He claims to be: the Savior of the world. He is the Bible's main character; He dominates every page of Scripture. And He is compelling. No man could have invented the story of Jesus. It's too fascinating. Too rich. Too miraculous.

Jesus is the ultimate reason that Christians follow the Bible. Only there can you and I learn about Him. Truth surrounds His actions and words. His power is unmistakable. He is more real than reality itself.

## ACCEPTING THE CONSEQUENCES OF DISENTANGLEMENT

If you realize you need to disentangle from a fear-based system and look to Scripture alone for guidance, there will most likely be consequences. This is often why disentangling can be so difficult. Someone who is part of a tight-knit religious community knows they will lose relationships if they question what everyone around them believes.

People who come to Christ from a religious system that shuns those who leave have sacrificed everything to follow Jesus. They are living examples of what Jesus said in Luke 14:26–27: "If anyone comes to me and does not hate his own father and mother and wife and children and brothers and sisters, yes, and even his own life, he cannot be my disciple. Whoever does not bear his own cross and come after me cannot be my disciple."

Thankfully, my self-denial doesn't look like losing my life. I'm not at risk of arrest because I've spoken out against Bill Gothard, his principles, and the IBLP ministry. I also don't think I will lose relationships with my family. I'm thankful for them and pray we will grow even closer in the coming years.

Still, I know that by rejecting the teaching of the community that raised me, I may lose influence. I may not be invited to events and into homes. Some may not appreciate that I'm speaking out on this topic. Others could assume the worst of my motives, or they will say that my husband, Jeremy, is to blame. They'll say I should never have married an outsider, a man who, though a Christian and a pastor, didn't believe all the same things I grew up believing. They will assume he convinced me to change my beliefs. While Jeremy walked with me through this journey, he always pointed me back to God's Word. And those words changed my heart. All Jeremy did was encourage me to examine Scripture, think for myself, and come to my own conclusions. Yet no matter how much I insist that this is my own journey, some won't be convinced that these are my convictions.

Whether you are deeply invested in a religious system or you have no religion, you will likely face the same criticism if you challenge your beliefs. So why do it? Why put yourself through all that conflict? Why sacrifice everything, or even something, in pursuit of the truth? For me, the answer is in Matthew 16. After Jesus talked about how His disciples must deny themselves to follow Him, He said, "For whoever would save his life will lose it, but whoever loses his life for my sake will find it. For what will it profit a man if he gains the whole world and forfeits his soul? Or what shall a person give in return for his soul?" (vv. 25–26). Add to that passage a verse that could be the theme of this book: John 8:32, which says, "You will know the truth, and the truth will set you free."

# PURSUING JESUS

So why is disentangling worth it? Because when you know the truth, you know Jesus. He is worth all the sacrifice. He brings freedom. He saves your soul. He makes you like Him and, after death, will bring you to eternity where you live with Him in heaven forever. He is far better than the relationships you may lose, the influence you may not have, or the community you leave behind.

In John 15, Jesus talked about what it's like to follow Him. My life is different, forever, because of this chapter, because I am not only a servant of Jesus. I am His friend.

> Greater love has no one than this, that someone lay down his life for his friends. You are my friends if you do what I command you. No longer do I call you servants, for the servant does not know what his master is doing; but I have called you friends, for all that I have heard from my Father I have made known to you (vv. 13–15).

Disentangling your beliefs can be a lonely task. It's easy to second-guess decisions, to wonder if you are doing it right. There will be times when it feels too difficult or complicated, and you will be tempted to give up. I've experienced all of that in recent years. I've felt lonely. Confused. Uncertain. During those moments, the truth in this passage was a life preserver. It kept me afloat as I went through the storms of change. It motivated me to keep disentangling for one simple reason: Jesus. Through my journey of disentanglement, I've found my life becoming more and more intertwined with His. He has made what I've gone through in my life, and especially in recent years, worthwhile. As long as I stay by

Jesus' side, He promises I will bear spiritual fruit. He has promised to love me forever.

As I've spent more time with Jesus in recent years, reading the Bible, understanding that He is the main character, I've become more and more amazed that Jesus calls Himself my friend. *My friend*. I would be happy to be His slave. Serving Him would be enough. But as He said in John 15, He chose me for something far sweeter: friendship. And because Jesus is my friend, I can go to Him with all my questions, problems, concerns, and failures. He hears me and responds with love. He laid down His life for me. I know He also hears my prayers.

If the end of your disentangling journey is anything other than Jesus, you've done it wrong. If your life is centered on anything or anyone other than Him, then you need to start disentangling. As Paul said in Philippians 1:21, "To live is Christ, and to die is gain." Jesus is worth living and dying for.

## TRUSTING GOD

I've started the last leg of my disentangling journey, but I won't finish this part of the trip until I reach heaven. For the rest of my life, I will fight to trust God instead of myself. That doesn't come naturally for any of us. Especially not me. But in the end, it's what all of us must do. We can't trust in any person or religious system. We have to trust in God.

When life is difficult, as it inevitably will be, we need to understand that God has a good reason for allowing us to suffer. He also has promised to be with us during the suffering. And when we are tempted to doubt our faith, we can't look to ourselves for assurance that we are on the right path. We have to look to God's character and the Bible's meaning to figure out the next right step.

In the end, that's all disentanglement is: trusting God and taking the next step in the right direction. As you untangle the lies from the truth, Christ will be there with you, keeping you by His side until He calls you home.

# Notes

## Chapter 1

1. "Free Jinger History," Free Jinger, accessed August 25, 2022, https://www.freejinger.org/help/free-jinger-history/.
2. Joshua Bote, "He wrote the christian case against dating. Now he's splitting from his wife and faith," *USA Today*, July 29, 2019, https://www.usatoday.com/story/news/nation/2019/07/29/joshua-harris-i-kissed-dating-goodbye-i-am-not-christian/1857934001.
3. Carly Mayberry, "Josh Harris Launches Course on Deconstructing Faith, but Some Theologians Question His Motives," *Newsweek*, August 13, 2021, https://www.newsweek.com/josh-harris-launches-course-deconstructing-faith-some-theologians-question-his-motives-1619263.

## Chapter 2

1. John MacArthur, "The Conscience, Revisited," Grace to You, accessed August 24, 2022, https://www.gty.org/library/articles/A273/the-conscience-revisited; emphasis in original.
2. "Bill Gothard," Institute in Basic Life Principles, accessed August 24, 2022, https://iblp.org/about-iblp/iblp-history/bill-gothard.
3. "IBLP History," Institute in Basic Life Principles, accessed August 24, 2022, https://iblp.org/about-iblp/iblp-history.

4. "The GOTHARD Files: The Early Years, 1965–79," Recovering Grace, February 11, 2014, https://www.recoveringgrace.org/2014/02/the-gothard-files-the-early-years-1965-79/.

5. Bill Gothard, "How to Trace Problems to Root Causes" (Basic Seminar Session 01, Institute in Basic Life Principles), MP4, 33:57, https://basicseminar.com/session/basic-seminar-session-01-how-to-trace-problems-to-root-causes/.

6. Gothard, 1:22.

7. Embassy University, *Four Secrets That Guarantee Success in Your Life! . . . And Your World!*, BillGothard.com, https://billgothard.com/resources/28-four-secrets-that-will-transform-your-life-and-your-world/.

## Chapter 3

1. Bill Gothard, *Questions and Answers on Infertility and Birth Control*, Basic Care Booklet 19 (Medical Training Institute of America), 41–42.

2. Gothard, 42–43.

3. Jim Sammons, "Session 20: Prepare Now for a Lasting Heritage" (Financial Freedom Seminar, Embassy Media), MP4, 44:32, https://embassymedia.com/media/session-20-prepare-now-lasting-heritage.

4. Sammons, 45:39.

5. John Piper, "Is It Wrong to Use Birth Control?" Desiring God, March 5, 2008, https://www.desiringgod.org/interviews/is-it-wrong-to-use-birth-control.

6. Matt Perman, "Does the Bible Permit Birth Control?" Desiring God, January 23, 2006, https://www.desiringgod.org/articles/does-the-bible-permit-birth-control.

7. Eric Roth, *Forrest Gump*, screenplay (1992), based on a novel by Winston Groom, http://www.dailyscript.com/scripts/forrest_gump.html.

8. "What Are the Seven Basic Life Principles?" Institute in Basic Life Principles, accessed August 24, 2022, https://www.iblp.org/questions/what-are-seven-basic-life-principles.

9. "What Are the Seven Basic Life Principles?"

10. Bill Gothard, *Seminar Workbook*, Session 1 (1996; repr., Hinsdale, IL: Institute in Basic Life Principles, 2006), 6, https://embassymedia.com/media/session-01-how-trace-problems-root-causes.

11. Gothard, 6.
12. Gothard, 6.
13. Gothard, 6.
14. Bill Gothard, *Seminar Workbook*, Session 14 (1996; repr., Oak Brook, IL: Institute in Basic Life Principles, 2006), 64, https://embassymedia.com/media/session-14-how-experience-gods-guarantee-success.
15. Gothard, "How to Trace Problems to Root Causes" (Basic Seminar Session 01), 53:36.
16. Bill Gothard, "Seven Universal Principles Taught in the Basic Seminar," BillGothard.com, accessed August 24, 2022, https://billgothard.com/teachings/.
17. "How 'Counseling Sexual Abuse' Blames and Shames Survivors," Recovering Grace, April 18, 2013, https://www.recoveringgrace.org/2013/04/how-counseling-sexual-abuse-blames-and-shames-survivors/.
18. Bill Gothard, "How to Overcome Self-Rejection" (Basic Seminar Session 02, Institute in Basic Life Principles), MP4, 39:26, https://basicseminar.com/session/basic-seminar-session-02-how-to-overcome-self-rejection/.
19. Gothard, 40:07.
20. Gothard, 45:58.
21. Bill Gothard, *Men's Manual*, vol. 1 (1979; repr., Hinsdale, IL: Institute in Basic Life Principles, Inc., 1993), 6.
22. John MacArthur, "Reasons to Forgive, Part 1," Grace to You, accessed August 25, 2022, https://www.gty.org/library/sermons-library/90-393/reasons-to-forgive-part-1.
23. Gothard, *Seminar Workbook*, Session 1, 6.
24. Bill Gothard, "Dealing with Hurts / Keys to Forgiveness" (Basic Seminar Session 07, Institute in Basic Life Principles), MP4, 22:43, https://basicseminar.com/session/basic-seminar-session-07-dealing-with-hurts-keys-to-forgiveness/.
25. Gothard, "How to Trace Problems to Root Causes" (Basic Seminar Session 01), 18:46.
26. Austin Duncan, "The Calm Before the Storm," Crossroads ministry sermon (Sun Valley, CA: Grace Community Church, January 20, 2019), 29:35, 31:31, 33:29, https://www.gracechurch.org/sermons/15264.

27. Bill Gothard, *Research in Principles of Life: Advanced Seminar Textbook* (Oak Brook, IL: Institute in Basic Youth Conflicts, 1986), 297.

28. "What Is an 'Umbrella of Protection'?" Institute in Basic Life Principles, accessed August 25, 2022, https://iblp.org/questions /what-umbrella-protection.

## Chapter 4

1. Bill Gothard, "How to Relate to Four Authorities" (Basic Seminar Session 04, Institute in Basic Life Principles), MP4, 00:38, https://basicseminar.com/session/ basic-seminar-session-04-how-to-relate-to-four-authorities/.

2. Bill Gothard, *Research in Principles of Life: Advanced Seminar Textbook* (Oak Brook, IL: Institute in Basic Youth Conflicts, 1986), 20.

3. Gothard, 25.

4. Bill Gothard, "Abnormal Social Development" (Basic Seminar Session 03, Institute in Basic Life Principles), MP4, 23:17, https://basicseminar.com/session/ basic-seminar-session-03-abnormal-social-development/.

5. Peter Hastie, "The Fear of God: Talking with Jerry Bridges," *Briefing*, September 1, 2002, http://thebriefing.com.au/2002/09/ the-fear-of-god-talking-with-jerry-bridges.

6. Gothard, *Research in Principles of Life: Advanced Seminar Textbook*, 297.

7. Amy McKenna, ed., "Jim Jones," *Encyclopaedia Britannica Online*, last updated May 9, 2022, https://www.britannica.com/biography/ Jim-Jones.

## Chapter 5

1. Jana, Jill, Jessa, and Jinger Duggar, *Growing Up Duggar: It's All About Relationships* (New York: Howard Books, 2014).

2. Duggar, 185, 187.

## Chapter 6

1. Bill Gothard, "How to Prepare Your Home for Successful Living" (Basic Seminar Session 12, Institute for Basic Life Principles, MP4) 1:17:38.
2. Bill Gothard, "The Development of Reprobation" (Basic Seminar Session 09, Institute in Basic Life Principles), MP4, 1:02:50, https://basicseminar.com/session/basic-seminar-session-09-the-development-of-reprobation/.
3. Bill Gothard, "How to Overcome Self-Rejection," 46:16.
4. Gothard, 46:56.
5. Bill Gothard, *Concepts for Anger Resolution*, Protect 4, series 2 (Basic Care Bulletin), 129.
6. Bill Gothard, "How to Trace Problems to Root Causes," (Basic Seminar Session 01, Institute for Basic Life Principles, MP4) 53:37.

## Chapter 7

1. "What Is a 'Rhema'?" Institute in Basic Life Principles, accessed August 27, 2022, https://iblp.org/questions/what-rhema.
2. Bill Gothard, *Life Purpose: A Journal of God's Power in Us*, vol. 1 (Oak Brook, IL: Institute in Basic Life Principles, 1990), 11.
3. Bill Gothard, Basic Care Bulletin 5, Medical Training Institute of America, *How to Make Wise Decisions on Adoption*, 40.

## Chapter 8

1. J. I. Packer, *Evangelical Magazine* 7 (Charleston, SC: BiblioLife, 2015), 19–20, self-quoted in *Knowing God* (1973; repr., Downers Grove, IL: InterVarsity Press, 1993), 201.
2. Packer, *Knowing God*, 202.
3. *The Overlooked Requirements for Riches, Honor and Life*, Supplementary Alumni Book, vol. 13 (Oak Brook, IL: Institute in Basic Youth Conflicts, 1987), 13.

## Chapter 9

1. Bill Gothard, Basic Seminar Session 04, *How to Relate to Four Authorities*, MP4, 46:54.

## Chapter 10

1. Steve Perisho, "A Common Quotation from 'Augustine'?" Georgetown University, accessed August 27, 2022, https://faculty .georgetown.edu/jod/augustine/quote.html.
2. Bill Gothard, Basic Care Bulletin 5, Medical Training Institute of America, *How to Make Wise Decisions on Adoption*, 28.

## Chapter 11

1. Jimmy and Clara Hinton, "Episode 198: Gothard's Girls—Charis Barker's Experience as a Survivor," April 28, 2022, in *Speaking Out on Sex Abuse*, podcast, YouTube video, 10:44, https://youtu.be /PTDIzjktZvo.
2. Bryan Smith, "The Cult Next Door," *Chicago*, June 20, 2016, https:// www.chicagomag.com/Chicago-Magazine/July-2016/Institute-in -Basic-Life-Principles-Hinsdale/.
3. Rachel Frost, quoted in Smith, "The Cult Next Door."
4. Hinton, "Episode 198: Gothard's Girls," 9:40.
5. Sarah Pulliam Bailey, "New Charges Allege Religious Leader, Who Has Ties to the Duggars, Sexually Abused Women," *Washington Post*, January 6, 2016, https://www.washingtonpost.com/news/acts -of-faith/wp/2016/01/06/new-charges-allege-religious-leader-who -has-ties-to-the-duggars-sexually-abused-women/.
6. "Statement from Recovering Grace Regarding the Lawsuit Against Bill Gothard and IBLP," Recovering Grace, March 28, 2018, https:// www.recoveringgrace.org/2018/03/statement-from-recovering -grace-regarding-the-lawsuit-against-bill-gothard-and-iblp/.
7. Board of Directors, "Statement Regarding Resignation," Institute in Basic Life Principles, March 17, 2014, https://iblp.org/news /statement-regarding-resignation.
8. Board of Directors, "A Time of Transition," Institute in Basic Life Principles, June 17, 2014, https://iblp.org/news/time-transition.
9. Bailey, "New Charges Allege Religious Leader."
10. "The GOTHARD Files: The Early Years, 1965–79," Recovering Grace, February 11, 2014, https://www.recoveringgrace.org/2014 /02/the-gothard-files-the-early-years-1965-79/.

11. "The GOTHARD Files: The Scandal, 1980," Recovering Grace, February 20, 2014, https://www.recoveringgrace.org/2014/02 /the-scandal-1980/.

12. "The GOTHARD Files: The Scandal."

13. Bailey, "New Charges Allege Religious Leader."

14. "Statement from Recovering Grace Regarding the Lawsuit."

15. Bill Gothard, "How False Accusations 'Worked Together for Good,'" BillGothard.com, accessed August 27, 2022, https://billgothard.com /testimonies/.

16. Gothard, "How False Accusations."

17. Bailey, "New Charges Allege Religious Leader."

18. Gothard, "How to Relate to Four Authorities," 55:51.

19. Smith, "The Cult Next Door," paragraph 31.

## Chapter 12

1. Abigail van Buren (Pauline Phillips), "Sinners and Saints!" Dear Abby, *Park City Daily News*, March 29, 1964, https://news.google .com/newspapers?nid=1697&dat=19640329&id=X-UeAAAAIBAJ&sji d=CUYEAAAAIBAJ&pg=7180,2561935&hl=en.

2. Austin Duncan, "Are You Stricter than Jesus?" Crossroads ministry sermon (Sun Valley, CA: Grace Community Church, June 5, 2022), https://www.gracechurch.org/sermons/19876.

## Chapter 13

1. Bill Gothard, "Why So Many Teens Join a Cult," BillGothard.com, accessed August 28, 2022, https://billgothard.com/teachings/.

2. Gothard, "Why So Many Teens."

# Acknowledgments

*This acknowledgment page* exists because of my friend Corey Williams. Corey, I don't know if you knew what you were getting into when you said you'd help me with this book! Neither did your wife, Kylie. You have both sacrificed so much. Thank you. Corey, you poured your heart and soul into this project, giving untold hours to helping me write and edit this manuscript on a tight timeline. I'm surprised that you still won't drink coffee.

To my husband, Jeremy: Thank you for being present, encouraging me when I've been down, and letting me cry on your shoulder. Writing this book has been an emotion-filled experience. You've been a gentle guide through times of confusion. Your often-daily reminders of God's love and care for me reflect your own. Knowing that I have your support means the world. I love you forever.

My precious daughters, Felicity Nicole and Evangeline Jo, I want you to know that everything I do, I do thinking of you. I love you and so does Jesus.

Oh, and special thanks to *CoComelon*—you really came in clutch.

Micah, you (with a bit of help from Stephen) fought off an overzealous security guard to capture the cover photo we needed. Well done.

So, a short story: Several days before the photo shoot for the book cover, I realized I didn't have anything to wear. Of course, I panicked. But then I found Ainyne Aiken! Ainyne, thank you for not only being available last-minute but for being a ridiculously talented stylist. You made me feel confident and comfortable.

Carolina, your hair-and-makeup skills are not the only assets you brought to the photo shoot. Your spunk and humor kept me laughing, even when I should've been focusing, but you made up for it with your helpful posing tips. You're the best.

To Stephanie Newton, who believed that my story needed to be told, thank you for giving me the platform to speak it. Your passion for the Lord is inspiring, and your patience with me is humbling. Thanks for all the deadline extensions! Also, many thanks to the amazing team at W Publishing Group: Lauren Bridges, Ashley Reed, Allison Carter, and Caren Wolfe.

My agent, Bryan Norman, who has a seemingly supernatural ability to never get stressed out, made this process as smooth as it could possibly be. Thanks, Bryan.

I'd like to mention and thank my pastors, John MacArthur and Austin T. Duncan, as well. Every week you faithfully show me Jesus Christ in all of His glory.

And it is to Jesus Christ, my kind and gracious Lord and Savior, that I owe my greatest gratitude and worship. "From him and through him and to him are all things. To him be glory forever. Amen" (Romans 11:36).

# About the Authors

**Jinger Duggar Vuolo** grew up on television. The daughter of Jim Bob and Michelle Duggar, she appeared on TLC's hit reality shows *19 Kids and Counting* and *Counting On* from the age of ten until she was twenty-seven. She is the author of several books, including *The Hope We Hold*, which she wrote with her husband, Jeremy, and the *New York Times* bestseller *Growing Up Duggar*, which she wrote with her sisters Jana, Jill, and Jessa. She now lives in Los Angeles, California, with her husband and their two daughters, Felicity Nicole and Evangeline Jo.

**Corey Williams** is the chief communications officer at the Master's Seminary in Sun Valley, California. He received a bachelor of arts in English from Clearwater Christian College and a master of arts in English literature from California State University at Northridge. He and his wife, Kylie, live in Santa Clarita, California, with their four children, Wade, Oakley, Lila, and Daisey.